WHEN THEY WERE GIRLS

By
REBECCA DEMING MOORE

ILLUSTRATED BY
MABEL BETSY HILL

EDITED BY
HELEN MILDRED OWEN

F. A. OWEN PUBLISHING COMPANY
DANSVILLE, NEW YORK

CONTENTS

EDITOR'S INTRODUCTION

When They Were Girls contains the stories of a group of American women, each one of whom occupies a very important place in her particular field. The stories of these women have been written many times before. We feel, however, that in this book you possibly may find that their stories have been written in a little different way. Our desire has been to bring very closely to the attention of our many readers some of the outstanding characteristics in the girlhoods of these women, and to show the relationship between these qualities in girlhood and the achievements of adult life.

To many people, doubtless to almost everyone, comes the desire to produce results, to achieve, and to add one's bit to the welfare of the world. Sometimes one is apt to become impatient, and to feel that he is not arriving at his goal. Under such circumstances it is helpful for us to acquaint ourselves with the life story of someone who we feel has reached the goal for which we are striving. We may then learn that success does not come overnight, but that years of careful, painstaking work are often spent before the contribution that one has for the world is completed.

It is so easy to admire someone who has attained success, and to wish for that same success and recognition oneself. Often, however, we are not willing to pay the price that he or she paid. To very few people does success come easily. The small minority to whom it does seem to come in that way can only remain successful through careful, painstaking work.

The women whose stories are within this book have not obtained the praise of the world easily. As girls, some of them were wealthy, some of them were very poor; but they *all* had obstacles to overcome. Each one had her own way to make. No amount of money, nor an especially fine environment, could ever be the means of making anyone successful. Success comes not from without, but from within.

It is, of course, desirable to have every opportunity that will help to develop one's particular ability. The greater a person's opportunity to receive help from all available good sources, the better it is for him. However, success depends upon oneself. No amount of encouragement, no effort put forth by loving parents, no amount of money expended for advantageous purposes, will ever accomplish great things unless the person himself really desires to achieve.

No matter how small our part in the world may seem, it is possible for us each to do our work in such a way that it will prove to be a forerunner of greater things to come. We can take but one step at a time, and by taking that step as best we know how we shall be led to something higher. In reading the stories in this book you will see at once that when these women were girls they had no idea of what they would ultimately achieve. Nevertheless, they each took the steps that seemed necessary to their progress, as each step presented itself. This careful preparation, this conscientious work, has enabled these women to give to the world their best, and has made it possible for us to profit not only by their gifts but by their example, as well.

HELEN MILDRED OWEN.

ROCHESTER, NEW YORK,
November 28, 1923.

WHEN THEY WERE GIRLS

JANE ADDAMS—
THE GIRL WHO BECAME A NEIGHBOR
TO THE NEEDY

"WHY do people live in such horrid little houses so close together, Father?" asked seven-year-old Jane on a trip to the city.

At home in the village, when she was tired of playing in the big roomy house, she could run across the green to the stream by her father's mill. Here, in the city, instead of wide green slopes and the low hum of the sawmill were narrow, dirty alleys and the clatter of carts and street cars.

When Mr. Addams explained that some people do not have money enough to choose pleasant places for their homes, Jane declared: "When I grow up, I shall have a large house, of course, but I shall not have it among other fine houses, but right in the midst of horrid little houses like these."

Now, strangely enough, when she grew up, she did that very thing. She went to live in a big house situated in the midst of poor Chicago tenements. Later, this little girl, who was Jane Addams, became known all over the world as the friend of the poor.

Jane Addams was born at Cedarville, Illinois, September 6, 1860. Little Jane could not remember her mother, who died when she was a baby, but she thought that no little girl ever had a father like hers. She was proud of his imposing figure, and she loved him dearly. Though he was a very busy man he always had time to answer her questions. She had a great many to ask, too, for even as a small child she did a good deal of thinking.

Jane's father had been a state senator for sixteen years and could tell her interesting stories about the history of the country. He talked to her so often about Abraham Lincoln, who had been his friend, that Jane felt almost as if she herself had known the great-hearted man.

One Sunday Jane appeared before her father dressed for Sunday school in a beautiful new coat. It was a finer coat than any other little girl in the village had. For this reason, Mr. Addams suggested that Jane wear her old coat to save the feelings of the other little girls. Jane consented to do so, although she was very much disappointed.

As they walked to Sunday school, Jane wondered how the good things of life could be more evenly divided. Ever since she had first seen the "horrid little houses" about a year before, her young mind had been busy with this problem. Jane turned to her father and asked him how it could be solved. He explained that even though everything cannot be divided evenly, people should act and dress in such a way that those who are less fortunate will not be made to feel so. He told her that in school and church, at least, people should be able to feel that they belong to one family.

Jane Addams attended the village school, and later, at seventeen years of age, entered Rockford Seminary, at Rockford, Illinois. Soon after she was graduated from this school it was declared a college, and she received the degree of B. A.

She had intended after her graduation to study medicine and to help the poor, but she was urged to go abroad because she was in poor health. While in London and elsewhere, she was greatly distressed by the wretched condition of the poor. Now she was more determined than ever to go about the work of helping others.

Miss Addams believed that it is better to show people how to help themselves than to give them gifts of money. "It is hard to help people one does not know," she reasoned, "and how can one really know people without seeing them very often?" True to the decision she had made as a child, she resolved to live among the poor and be a real neighbor to them.

With the help of some friends, Miss Addams opened Hull-House, which is located in a tenement section of Chicago. Here, she established a day nursery where mothers who had to go out to work could leave their babies in good care. A kindergarten was organized for the young children in the neighborhood.

There are clubs for girls and boys, and also for men and women. Classes in sewing, cooking, and millinery are conducted for the girls. "The Young Heroes," a boy's club, today has for its own use a five-story building equipped with recreation and study rooms. Printing, photography, and many other trades can be learned there. Hull-House, originally occupying one building, is now using thirteen buildings, each fitted for some special service.

For more than thirty years Miss Addams

and her fellow-workers have stood ready to do any neighborly act, from bathing little babies to teaching and entertaining lonely old women. At Hull-House a cordial welcome always awaits everyone.

Besides her friendly aid to those who flock to Hull-House, Jane Addams has been a good neighbor to people whom she has never seen. She helped to have a law passed in Illinois to prevent children who are under fourteen years of age from working in factories. Through her efforts public baths have been provided in Chicago. Remembering the merry games she played as a child on the river banks near her home, she has made many a plea for more playgrounds for city girls and boys.

Miss Addams has been a member, often the chairman, of many important committees that have been organized to plan ways for making the world a better place in which to live. She has also found time to write books on this subject.

Jane Addams might have given money to

the poor and spent her time in travel and amusement, but she preferred to give herself. Because she loves people enough to learn what they really need and works *with* them as well as *for* them, thousands bless her as a true friend and neighbor.

LOUISA M. ALCOTT—
WHOSE STORIES OF REAL LIFE ARE
A DELIGHT TO GIRLS AND BOYS

WHEN Louisa Alcott peeped into her journal on the morning of her tenth birthday, she found a little note from her mother filled with loving messages. It read: "I give you the pencil-case I promised, for I have observed that you are fond of writing, and wish to encourage the habit."

Louisa's mother often wrote little messages in her daughter's journal, urging her to keep on trying to be good. Very often the notes encouraged Louisa to go on writing.

On both her fourteenth and fifteenth birthdays her mother's gift was a pen, with a poem and a loving letter.

As Louisa, at eight years of age, had written a little verse about a robin, Mrs. Alcott hoped that her daughter would some day be a great writer. It was a hope that was realized, for Louisa M. Alcott's books have become famous, delighting each succeeding generation.

Little Women, her first great success, is the story of the Alcott family. It tells of their jolly times and their hard times at the Orchard House at Concord, Massachusetts. The lively outspoken "Jo" of the story, writing in the attic, is Louisa herself; the other "March" girls are her own dear sisters, Anna, Elizabeth, and Abba May. "Marmee," of course, is the beloved mother, and Mr. March, the father.

Louisa May Alcott was born at Germantown, Pennsylvania, November 29, 1832, but most of her girlhood was spent in Boston and Concord, Massachusetts. It was a happy

life that she led even though the food was
plain and her clothes were generally "made
over." There was never enough money to go
around in the Alcott family, but there was
no lack of love, kindness, good conversation,
and good reading.

Louisa and her sisters received their education chiefly from their father, a man of
rare intellect. Mr. Alcott was devoted to his
children and he took great pleasure in teaching them. In addition to these daily lessons
there often were long, hard tasks of sewing
and ironing, but there was plenty of time for
play, too.

What fun they had! In the old barn at
Concord with their playmates, the children
of Ralph Waldo Emerson and of Nathaniel
Hawthorne, they acted out their favorite
fairy tales and also *The Pilgrim's Progress*.
Their giant tumbled off the loft when Jack
cut down the bean stalk, and there was a real
pumpkin for Cinderella's coach.

Their mother's birthday was always a
great event. When that day arrived Louisa

would say to herself as soon as she awoke, "It's Mother's birthday: I must be very good." After breakfast the children always gave their mother her presents. One year Louisa's gift was a cross made of moss with a bit of poetry attached. That day there were no lessons, and everybody was very jolly and happy.

Two great joys of Louisa's life were books and the outdoors. She enjoyed a quiet corner with a good book. She also loved to run in the woods in the early morning before the dew was off the grass. She liked to feel the velvety moss under her feet and to look up into the green branches overhead. Once, when she was a child, she paused in her running and stood still listening to the rustle of the pines.

"It seemed as if I *felt* God," she wrote in her journal, "and I prayed in my heart that I might keep that happy sense of nearness all my life."

Louisa had a quick temper and found difficulty in managing it. At fourteen years of age she wrote a poem about her struggles en-titled, "My Little Kingdom." It began:

"A little kingdom I possess,
    Where thoughts and feelings dwell.
And very hard I find the task
    Of governing it well;
For passion tempts and troubles me,
    A wayward will misleads,
And selfishness its shadow casts
    On all my words and deeds."

She kept on trying, however, and never let her little kingdom control her.

As Louisa Alcott grew older she began to realize very keenly all the cares that burden-ed the dear "Marmee" because of their lack of money. None of Mr. Alcott's ventures in teaching or lecturing had added much to the family treasury.

Louisa was determined to help and she willingly did any kind of work that would en-able her to earn a little money for her dear ones. Sometimes she taught school, some-times she helped a relative with the house-work, and sometimes she took care of an in-valid child. Often she did fine needlework.

While her hands were busy with her daily tasks, her brain was active planning stories. She wrote them late at night, and soon publishers began to accept them and pay her small sums of money. For her first story, written when she was sixteen years old, she was paid five dollars.

Writing was a joy to Louisa Alcott and sewing a tiresome task. However, she continued her sewing because at first the needle paid better than the pen. It was a pleasure to her to earn enough money to buy a new shawl for "Marmee," a crimson ribbon for May's bonnet, or a new carpet for the whole family. Cheerfully she wore her old bonnet and her shabby shoes.

During her spare moments, the young author continued to write happily in her attic. To her delight the mail often brought her the news that her stories had been accepted. This greatly encouraged her.

Then came the Civil War. Louisa realized that no matter how greatly she desired to write, her first duty was to her country.

Therefore, she went to the Union Hotel Hospital at Georgetown, D. C., as a nurse. The letters that she wrote home telling of her experiences were later published as a book called *Hospital Sketches*.

By this time Miss Alcott's work had become so well known that she was asked to write a book for girls. She began to write *Little Women* to prove to the publisher that she could not write for girls. What she did prove everybody knows. Young people and their elders as well, not only in this country but also abroad, were soon laughing and crying over the doings of the "March" girls. Miss Alcott had become famous.

Little Men and other books followed rapidly and proved so popular that Miss Alcott received many thousands of dollars from her writings. She was happy because now she could fulfill her dream of giving her dear mother some of the comforts that she had never had. It was but small return, she felt, for all the help and encouragement that her mother had given her.

Miss Alcott's books have lived because they show people as they really are. They tell, too, how jolly and happy life can be if people think less about money and more about living unselfishly and enjoying the outdoors and the simple and beautiful things of life. Louisa M. Alcott could not help writing in this way, for it was the way in which she herself lived.

SUSAN B. ANTHONY —
WHO WORKED FOR SIXTY YEARS TO SECURE
RIGHTS FOR WOMEN

YOUNG Susan vigorously attacked, with her broom, the cobweb in the corner of the schoolroom ceiling. It was a stubborn cobweb and Susan had to step upon the teacher's desk to reach it. No girl trained by so good a housekeeper as Susan's mother could be happy in the same room with a cobweb.

"Deborah will be pleased to have the room clean," thought Susan. However, Deborah, her Quaker teacher, was not pleased. Su-

san's heavy shoes had broken the desk
hinges, and the girl who had tried to do well
was severely scolded.

It was often very much like this in Susan
B. Anthony's later life. When she tried her
hardest to brush away the cobwebs that kept
the world from seeing that women did not
have the same rights as men, she was jeered
and scorned. Nevertheless, she kept on
wielding her broom, the broom she used being her clever tongue. This little Quaker
girl grew up to be an interesting and elo-
quent lecturer, who never lost an opportunity to speak a good word for her fellow-
women.

Susan Brownell Anthony was born February 15, 1820, in Adams, Massachusetts,
in the midst of the Berkshire Hills. She
was the second of eight children. Every
night, as a little girl, she used to watch the
sun go down behind "Old Greylock." She
came to love the great mountain, and all her
life she liked to think of its rugged strength.

Mrs. Anthony was a very busy woman. In

addition to caring for her lively little children she also cooked and washed for a number of factory hands. However, she found time to read good books and to be interested in all her children's doings. Susan's father was a Quaker, a man much liked and respected.

At an early age little Susan learned to be a good cook and housekeeper, like her mother. Once, when Mrs. Anthony was ill, twelve-year-old Susan with the help of her two sisters, ten and fourteen years of age, did all the household tasks, including packing the lunch boxes for the factory hands. Susan was so anxious that everything should be done exactly right that she and her sisters carried samples of the food to their mother for her approval.

At three years of age Susan, who was very bright and quick, learned her letters and also some words, while on a visit at her grandmother's. When she was a little older she attended a district school, and then a private school conducted in the Anthony home.

Later, she joined her sister at a boarding school near Philadelphia, where she studied for a year.

Susan began to teach in a district school when she was seventeen years old. She was boarded in turn at the homes of her pupils, being paid in addition only one dollar and a half a week. Susan was a very successful teacher, and often she grew indignant to see that men who did not do their work so well as she received four times as much pay. Equal pay for equal work was one of the rights that she began to demand for her fellow-women from that time on.

When Susan's father failed in business, she saw his creditors take all of her mother's personal things. Susan was enraged with the injustice of it and declared that there should be a law to make a wife's belongings her own.

In 1851 Miss Anthony made a trip to Seneca Falls, New York, to urge the admission of girls to the People's College then being founded. There she met Miss Lucy

Stone and had an opportunity to become well acquainted with her and also with Mrs. Elizabeth Cady Stanton, whom she had met a few months before.

Mrs. Stanton and Miss Stone believed that women should have a share in making the laws of the land, and Miss Anthony soon became their most ardent co-worker. Twenty-five years later, Miss Anthony drafted the federal suffrage amendment. However, it was forty-five years from the time that the amendment was drafted until it became a part of our Constitution.

Susan B. Anthony was one of the greatest friends that women have ever had. When she was born there were only three things that a girl who wanted to earn her living could do: be a millhand, a servant, or a teacher. Before the close of Miss Anthony's life, a girl might fit herself to be a doctor, a lawyer, a business woman, or, in fact, almost anything that she chose.

When Miss Anthony was a young girl, the doors of nearly all colleges were closed to women. The girl who dared to ask for as much education as was given to her brother was considered a great oddity. However, Miss Anthony lived to see girls admitted to college quite as a matter of course.

Susan B. Anthony found a world where a married woman could not do what she liked with the property that she owned. Neither could she do as she wished with the money that she had earned or received as a gift. She could not even take charge of her own children if anyone objected. Miss Anthony left a world where women's rights in all these matters were considered and where in four states women could help to make the laws. The Nineteenth Amendment, giving women the vote, came later.

Miss Anthony devoted all of her time to public speaking. She traveled from coast to coast, always making the most of every opportunity to speak in behalf of the various reforms to which she devoted over sixty years of her life. Sometimes she pleaded for the freedom of the slaves, sometimes for temperance, but *always* for her favorite cause—rights for women.

Susan B. Anthony kept on pleading for women, no matter how much people laughed at her. Gradually, the world began to see some reason in what she said. To-day, all women who cast their vote, control their property, and send their daughters to college, can thank the determined Quaker girl who had such a large share in giving women their rights.

CLARA BARTON —
THE GIRL WHO UNFURLED
THE FIRST AMERICAN RED CROSS FLAG

THE Barton family was made very happy on the Christmas of 1821 with the gift of a baby girl. The four older sisters and brothers gave the baby a royal welcome, though they little thought that this gift was also to be a Christmas present to the whole world. This baby was Clara Barton, called in Civil War times the "Angel of the Battlefield," and known by all nations as the founder of the American Red Cross Society.

Baby Clara grew up to be the pet of the family, although no coddling was allowed on the Barton farm in Oxford, Massachusetts. Each member of the family wanted to teach her something, and Clara was equally eager to learn.

Mrs. Barton taught her daughter to be level headed. Nothing could have been worth more to the girl who was to be the first woman to carry organized aid to the wounded on an American battlefield. Mrs. Barton also taught Clara to sew, to cook, and to be an excellent housekeeper.

Clara was particularly grateful for this knowledge and had countless opportunities to use it. Once a dying soldier whispered his wish for a custard pie, crinkly around the edge, to remind him of home. With what materials she could get together, Miss Barton made the pie and scalloped the edge with her finger, just as her mother had taught her to do in the farm kitchen.

It was Big Brother David who taught the little sister many things that were to make her a very practical "Angel of the Battle-field." At five years of age, thanks to his training, she rode wild horses like a young Mexican. This skill in managing any horse meant the saving of countless lives when she had to gallop all night in a trooper's saddle to reach the wounded men. David taught her, also, to drive a nail straight, to tie a knot that would hold, and to think and act quickly.

From her father Clara heard thrilling tales of his fighting in the Revolutionary War under "Mad Anthony" Wayne. These stories doubtless made a deep impression on the youthful listener. Little did she realize that in the years to come she, too, would play an important part on many battlefields.

Clara Barton attended a boarding school for a short time. However, she received her education chiefly at home, being taught by her brother and then by a tutor. Later she had an opportunity for more advanced study at a near-by school.

The little farm girl was busy and happy

from morning until night, for she loved to do things. She went for the cows, helped with the milking and churning, and had a hand in planting the potatoes. When the house was being painted, she begged to help with that, too, and she learned how to mix the paint as well as to put it on. Once she went into her brother's factory and learned how to weave cloth.

Her first experience as a nurse came at the age of eleven when Big Brother David was injured by a fall. For two years this cheerful, patient little nurse scarcely left his. bedside.

When she was only fifteen years old, Clara Barton began to teach school. She taught well, too, for she understood girls and boys. It seemed as if she had found the work that she best liked to do. However, after eighteen years of teaching, her health necessitated her giving up this profession. Clara Barton did not know how to be idle, so she went to Washington and secured a position in the Patent Office.

When the Civil War broke out many wounded soldiers were brought to Washington. Clara Barton helped to care for these boys, some of whom were her former pupils from Massachusetts. She also sent out appeals for money and supplies.

As Miss Barton saw the wounded taken from the transports, she was extremely sorry for them because they did not have proper care. She felt that she must go to nurse the soldiers who were close to the battlefields. This was entirely against army regulations, but Miss Barton was very persistent. She was finally allowed to take her store of bandages and other supplies to the front, where they were most needed.

People used to ask Miss Barton if she had not always been brave. The woman who walked coolly through Fredericksburg when every street was a firing line answered, telling of her childhood: "I was a shrinking little bundle of fears—fears of thunder, fears of strange faces, fears of my strange self." It was when the shy girl forgot herself in working for others that she forgot her fears.

Bravery and willingness to help others, however, would have been of little use to Clara Barton had she not been level headed. The ability to see what should be done next and to do it quickly and well were of equal value. It seemed as if Clara Barton worked magic, but her magic was only a mixture of common sense and a great pity for the suffering.

Once at Antietam, when there seemed to be nothing to feed to the wounded men, she noticed that the medicine had been packed in fine meal. Quickly she borrowed several big kettles from the farm where they were quartered, and she soon was serving the men with steaming gruel.

At another time, at nightfall, one of the doctors complained about the mismanagement that left him with a thousand wounded men to care for and only an inch of candle for a light. Miss Barton had fortunately brought along several boxes of lanterns, which she gave him. Her remarkable forethought meant the saving of many a life that night.

After the Civil War Clara Barton did not give up her work of mercy. For four years she helped to trace missing soldiers.

While in Europe, during the Franco-Prussian War, she saw the wonderful work that the Red Cross societies abroad were doing. She was deeply impressed with the value of such an organization and immediately decided that, upon her return to the United States, she would do all that she could to interest her country in the Red Cross.

Miss Barton worked for years to persuade the United States to found an American Red Cross Society. "We shall never have another war," people objected. However, Miss Barton pointed out that in time of great floods, fires, earthquakes, and other disasters lives could be saved by organized aid. At last she was successful, for in 1882 the American Red Cross Society came into being. Clara Barton was its president for many years.

The Red Cross banner was first unfurled for service in this country at Miss Barton's home at Dansville, New York, where she established a local chapter to aid the forest-fire sufferers in Michigan. Ever since that time the Red Cross has continued to give its efficient aid wherever needed. It had an exceptional opportunity during the World War to prove its worth. Our country has cause for deep gratitude to Clara Barton.

Clara Barton risked her life on sixteen battlefields of the Civil War to care for the wounded. She founded the organization that has brought relief to thousands of people in war and disaster. She did great deeds, but they were possible only because she had learned to do the little things of life well.

AMY MARCY CHENEY BEACH—
THE GIRL WHO MADE MELODIES

"SEE, the conquering hero comes" rang out in the studio, clear and true as a bell. The photographer thrust his head out from under the big black hood of the camera and stared in amazement at the tiny sitter. The two-year-old child was singing the very air that he had been practicing for the first peace jubilee, and she was singing it absolutely correctly. Others were eventually to be astonished at the musical ability of this little girl, who grew up to be America's foremost woman composer.

Amy Marcy Cheney was born in the little town of Henniker, New Hampshire, September 5, 1857. From the time that she was a year old, her talent amazed even her musical mother. She learned dozens of airs and sang them, keeping the pitch perfectly. She would listen delightedly for hours to violin music.

At the age of four Amy was finally allowed to play on the piano. Often when her aunt was seated at the instrument, little Amy would stand on a hassock and play with her, making up an accompaniment as she went along.

Just as other little girls plan how to arrange their playhouses or how to make new dresses for their dolls, this little girl used to think out tunes. Once, when she was visiting at a house where there was no piano, she composed a little piece of music. She remembered it and three months later was able to play it correctly on the piano at home. She had composed three other little pieces before she was seven years old.

Long before Amy knew the names of musical notes, she knew their meaning and could read them. It amused her to transpose from one key to another, and she never found it difficult.

When she was six years old Amy thought that she should have regular music lessons, so she begged her mother, who was an excellent pianist, to teach her. You may be sure that little Amy Cheney never had to be urged to practice. At seven years of age she played several times in public. Before long she was playing difficult music from Chopin, Bach, and other composers.

When Amy was eight years old her family moved to Boston. The prominent musicians of this city before whom she played agreed that she was ready to go to Europe to study music. However, Mr. and Mrs. Cheney did not want their little girl to be trained only in music. They knew that she would be happier and healthier if she were to go to school with children of her own age. They also realized that she should have plenty of time

to romp and play outdoors with other
children.

Amy was therefore sent to a private
school, conducted by Mr. W. L. Whittemore,
where she rapidly mastered the regular
studies. She was greatly helped in her piano
work by her good ear and accurate memory.
She was able to play a whole Beethoven sona-
ta without notes after she had heard one of
her fellow-pupils practice it.

While Amy was quite young her quick ear
and good memory gave her an opportunity
to be of real service to the world. Professor
Sill, a scientist who made birds his special
study, asked her to record the songs of the
California larks.

Out into the fields they went together and
waited, motionless, for the birds to appear.
Then just as soon as one of the little feath-
ered creatures trilled out his melody, Amy
wrote it down in notes. The song thus
caught was kept for all time. She continued
this practice of recording songs so that she
finally had a volume filled with bird melodies.

Amy Cheney studied under Ernst Perabo, Carl Baerman, and Junius W. Hill. She also studied many musical subjects independently. She did not always want to be helped over the problems that confronted her, preferring to work them out alone. Translating books on music and memorizing and rewriting difficult music were some of the hard tasks that this earnest, thorough young student set for herself.

At sixteen years of age this young pianist made her first professional appearance before the public at a recital in Boston, and was greatly praised. The next year she played with the Boston Symphony Orchestra and with the Theodore Thomas Orchestra. During that year a beautiful song which she had composed, entitled *With Violets*, was published. It was considered by musical critics to be faultless in form.

The following year Amy Cheney became the wife of Dr. H. H. A. Beach, of Boston. She did not, however, give up her musical career. In fact, all of her most important pieces of music were written after her marriage.

Mrs. Beach has composed music for the orchestra, piano, and violin, and has also written cantatas and many songs. One of her most famous and successful pieces of music is her *Jubilate* cantata, written for the dedication of the Woman's Building at the World's Columbian Exposition, held in Chicago in 1893. At this Exposition Maud Powell, the famous violinist, and Mrs. Beach played one of Mrs. Beach's compositions written for the violin and piano.

The music for a poem called *Dark Is the Night* is thought by many people to be her best song. Other favorites are: *Across the World, Scottish Cradle Song,* and *Fairy Lullaby.* Mrs. Beach's songs are always enjoyed by those who appreciate the best music.

Success did not spoil the young girl whose marked musical ability had attracted attention ever since her babyhood. Not content with what had come easily to her, Amy Marcy Cheney Beach kept on working to develop her talent. Her love of music and enthusiasm for it were not alone responsible for placing her foremost among the women composers of America. It was her desire for knowledge, leading her to studiously apply herself to her work, that enabled her to create music which has brought pleasure to thousands of people.

CECILIA BEAUX—
WHOSE PAINT BRUSH
HAS BROUGHT HER FAME

CECILIA'S gray eyes grew thoughtful as she considered the drawing that she was copying. She held it at arm's length, scrutinizing it critically.

"Ah, this is much more fun than practicing scales," she reflected.

When the family examined these drawings, they said, "Cecilia would never be a success at music, but she draws very well."

This little girl was Cecilia Beaux, whose portraits have won many medals. She was born in Philadelphia in 1863. Her father came from Provence, France, where the people have ever been famed for their enjoyment of beauty. Her mother was of New England descent and had inherited from her ancestors the ability to do things and to do them conscientiously and well.

From each parent the little girl received a golden gift: from her father, his joy in the beautiful; from her mother, the love of doing things. Her good use of these two gifts has made Cecilia Beaux a famous artist.

Cecilia was taught at home until she was twelve years old. Then she attended a private school for a short time. Because of the skill that she had shown in copying drawings her aunt and uncle, with whom she spent a great deal of time, proposed a training in art for her.

This young girl had a few lessons in drawing from a Philadelphia artist, Mrs. Thomas Janvier. She also had an opportunity to have her work in painting criticized by Mr. William Sartain. Her gray eyes shone with happiness as she applied her colors and listened eagerly to every word from this distinguished teacher. Cecilia Beaux was practically self-taught. These few lessons constituted her only instruction in art until she went abroad some years later.

Instead of sitting and dreaming of the great pictures that she might paint some day, Cecilia Beaux looked for an opportunity to use her brush or pencil to aid her financially. A scientific society needed some one upon whom they could depend to make accurate drawings of fossils. This kind of work necessitated very careful attention to detail. The drawings were to be made into plates to illustrate scientific books. They would have been useless if they had not been exactly correct.

Some young artists, eager to do what they would call big things, would have been impatient with such slow, tedious work. Cecilia Beaux did not despise it. She did it to the very best of her ability, just because she believed in doing things well. Little did she dream that this training in careful and exact drawing was to be of great help to her when she began to paint portraits.

Another way in which she earned money was by giving lessons in painting and drawing. She also found that she could increase her income by painting portraits on china plates, taking her subjects from photographs. She did these very well, too, being careful to make correct likenesses.

Then Cecilia Beaux began to make crayon portraits from photographs. These attracted attention and she soon received many orders for portraits.

One success followed another, but although Cecilia Beaux received much praise for her work, she was not content with what she had accomplished. She felt that she needed still more training and that to have it she must go to Paris.

Accordingly, Miss Beaux went to Europe and began to broaden her talent by studying with several great French masters. One of them, Robert Fleury, used to summon her

before the class to praise her work publicly.
So modest was this American girl that she
thought he could not be in earnest. Her fel-
low-students, also, used to discuss her excellent work.

The many friends that she made in Paris
begged her to stay in that beautiful city and
paint there, but she was too thoroughly
American to spend her life in a foreign land.
So, after a few years, she returned to her
own country.

A great many of Miss Beaux's best-known
pictures are of women and children, but she
has painted men with great success, too. In
fact, she was chosen to paint portraits of
Clemenceau, Admiral Beatty, and other
great war leaders. Her portraits of women
and children are really little pictures of
everyday home life. She has caught the
children as they have paused in their play
for a moment.

"Ernesta," one of Miss Beaux's well-known
portraits, hangs in the Metropolitan Museum
of Art in New York City. Among her other

important paintings are "The Last Days of Infancy," "The Dancing Lesson," "Sita and Sarita," and "The New England Woman."

Cecilia Beaux has won medals and prizes at many exhibitions of art. People are glad to pay large sums of money for her pictures, and it is considered an honor to be painted by her. She has steadily achieved success because she has never scorned nor slighted small tasks. She has done them conscientiously and well, making them a preparation for greater things to come.

EVANGELINE BOOTH —
THE GIRL WHO LIVED
THE MEANING OF HER NAME

MANY a passerby on the crowded London street paused to glance at the earnest, thoughtful face of a slender, golden-haired flower girl and to buy a nosegay from her basket. When her stock was sold this girl, as fair and fragile as one of her own flowers, picked her way through the throng. She presently disappeared into one of the dirty alleyways, where only the poorest of Londoners lived.

Children ran to meet her and rough men

touched their caps as she passed. The sick woman whose wretched room she entered fell asleep peacefully after receiving a bowl of soup from her hands and a cheery word.

For weeks this sweet-faced young girl, who sold flowers or worked at making matches, had been winning the hearts of the poor, discouraged people of this district. She tended their babies and prayed with the lonely old women. These people felt that they had found a friend who was sorry for them and who was always ready to give them aid. They called her the "White Angel."

One day she told these people that she was a Salvation Army lassie. The Army was hated in this district because it was trying to close the saloons; only a few months earlier its preachers had been stoned in the streets. The "White Angel," herself, had been warned by the police that it would be dangerous for her to speak in this part of London. Yet so beloved and respected had she become that she felt perfectly safe. Because of her good work, the people in this poverty-stricken and wicked district were soon attending the meetings of the Army.

The girl who dared to go into the very worst part of London to live the life of its poor people that she might better know how to help them was Evangeline Booth. In later years she became the Commander-in-chief of the Salvation Army in the United States.

Evangeline Booth's father, William Booth, had been apprenticed as a boy to a pawn-broker. He was so touched by the poverty and wickedness around him that he put his whole soul into helping others to lead better lives. The Mission, that he established in London after many struggles, became in time the Salvation Army. For years, William Booth, General of the Army, toiled against odds of every kind.

The thinking world now has respect and admiration for the splendid work that the Salvation Army carries on. In those days, however, the street preachers of the Army were as likely to be showered with stones and bricks as to be sneered and ridiculed. The rougher people disliked the Army because it was fighting drink and wickedness. Other people could not see that the drum and tambourine and simple prayers might help to turn a man's heart to God as readily as could organ music and learned sermons.

It was into the home of the founder of this once despised organization, at Hackney, a suburb of London, that a seventh child, Evangeline Booth, was born, December 25, 1865. There was a loving welcome for the little girl, though she had come into a home where both mother and father believed that their family must be second to the work that they were doing for the world.

Little Evangeline and her sisters heard so much of their father's work that even their favorite game was playing prayer meeting with their battered dolls. She and the others had very few toys, because their parents thought that the money should be spent for the poor.

It was a very busy home in which Eva, as

her father preferred to call her, grew up.
The bell was always ringing. Messengers
were coming and going. In one room her
father's deep voice might be heard planning
his work. In another room her mother was
busy writing for the Cause. The younger
children murmured their lessons in a third
room, and in a fourth, one of the older girls
practiced on the piano.

The General would often stop in the midst
of his work for little chats with his children.
He would take Eva, for whom he always had
a specially deep love and tenderness, upon
his knee and ask her about her puppies or
kittens. Once when Eva felt very sad over
the death of her pet dog, her father took her
to the city and spent the whole day telling
her stories and comforting her.

At an early age Eva learned that she
should pick up her books and toys for, above
everything else except sin, her father hated
disorder. Orderliness was a useful habit to
be acquired by one who was later to have
charge of the affairs of a great organization.

Though Eva's mother was often too busy to spend much time with her, she heard her daughter's prayers and urged her to study so that she could help the weak, the poor, the ignorant, and the wicked. Mrs. Booth often reminded Eva to carry out in her life the meaning of her beautiful name, Evangeline, "bringing glad tidings."

Evangeline Booth began her work of "bringing glad tidings" when she was very young. She had inherited her father's gift of eloquence as well as his fearlessness and love of work. At fifteen years of age she spoke very beautifully at a meeting near London. When she was seventeen years old she was made an officer in the Army and began the work in the slums which won her the title of "White Angel."

After ably filling various positions in the Salvation Army in Great Britain, Evangeline Booth was made Commander of the Army in Canada. At the time of the Gold Rush in 1898, she sent Salvation Army workers to the Klondike. In 1904 she was made

Commander-in-chief of the Salvation Army in the United States. Besides her duties as Commander she has composed words and music for the Army's songs and has written articles for the Army publications and other magazines.

In addition to its religious work the Salvation Army maintains homes, hospitals, clinics, and day nurseries; it finds employment for men and women out of work; and it sends mothers and children on summer outings. Every Christmas and Thanksgiving pennies dropped into the big red Salvation Army kettles provide dinners for thousands of the poor. In a single year the Army in the United States made 175,698 children happy with Christmas toys.

During the World War the pies and doughnuts served by the Salvation Army lassies cheered thousands of lonely soldiers, and many a mother has the Salvation Army to thank for her boy's last message.

Evangeline Booth was for almost twenty years Commander-in-chief of this great or-

ganization in the United States. She believes, as her father did before her, that the
first step in influencing a man to lead a better life is to make him feel that you really
care whether he sinks or swims. Her courageous, selfless life shows that she *does* care.

FRANCES HODGSON BURNETT—
THE GIRL WHO LOVED STORIES
AND WROTE THEM

FROM under the sitting-room table
came strange whispers, but Mrs.
Hodgson was not at all surprised.
Beneath the long overhanging cover she
could see a chubby, curly-headed little girl
seated on the floor talking in low earnest
tones to her wax doll, braced against the
table leg.

Frances, the little girl under the table,
would have described the scene very differ-
ently. What she saw was not an ordinary

center table, but an Indian wigwam; not a speechless doll, but a squaw to whom she, as the chief, was telling tales of the war-trail and the happy hunting grounds.

"Frances is pretending again," said Mrs. Hodgson to herself as she went out of the room, a bit puzzled at this little daughter's way of playing.

The chubby little girl and her doll had many an adventure together. They took mad gallops on coal-black steeds that seemed to ordinary eyes nothing but the arms of the nursery sofa. As survivors from a sinking ship they drifted on a raft that Frances' two sisters would have called the green arm chair. These experiences seemed very real to this little girl.

Something within little Frances' curly head helped her to transform the sitting-room cupboard into a temple in Central America and the stiff doll into Mary Queen of Scots. It was the gift of imagination. How surprised her family would have been at that time had they known that this gift was one day to make her a famous story-writer.

In the smoky factory town of Manchester, England, Frances Eliza Hodgson was born, November 24, 1849. When she was about four years old, her sweet, gentle mother was left a widow.

Like other English children of families in comfortable circumstances, the Hodgson girls had a governess at home, before they entered a near-by private school. The lessons which interested Frances the most were those that contained stories, such as certain parts of history. She could never satisfy her great appetite for stories, though she read continually.

There were not so many good books for children then as nowadays. Frances' relatives seemed to think that the birthday and Christmas gift books were quite enough for a little girl. Frances, however, did not agree with them. When she made a new acquaintance at school, she was sure to ask her, first of all, what books she had to lend. Sometimes when she went to visit a little friend, she forgot her manners entirely and buried herself in a new book, so eager was she to read.

One gloomy rainy day, Frances wandered through the house looking for something to read. She glanced at the tall secretary and wished that its books looked more interesting. However, she decided that she might at least try one. Accordingly, she pulled out a fat volume. It had short lines, which, to Frances, meant conversation and a story. She opened another book and found more stories. Delightedly, she continued to examine the books.

Frances was so excited and happy that she forgot to go to tea. She had discovered that there were stories enough to last her for months! It was in this way that Frances Hodgson discovered Shakespeare's plays, Scott's and Dickens' novels, and many other interesting books.

Not content with reading stories, Frances was always telling or writing them. On the afternoons at school when the girls were allowed to talk quietly over their crocheting and fancy work, Frances would tell stories in low tones to the group of girls near her. They were delighted with her tales and continually begged her to tell more.

At home she often wrote stories on slates or in old account books. For fear of being teased she rarely showed the stories to anyone except her mother. Mrs. Hodgson always had an encouraging word for her little daughter's tales and verses. This gave Frances an added incentive to continue writing.

Just at the close of the Civil War a great change came into the life of the little storywriter. Mrs. Hodgson decided to leave England and move to America. The family fortunes were impaired, and an uncle had promised to find work for the boys in the United States.

Romantic Frances was delighted with the change. Her first American home was in a tiny settlement in the forests of Tennessee Everything was so new and strange that she seemed actually to be living in a story. The next home on the top of a hill, with mountains in the distance, was even better. How she loved the bright sunshine, the flowers, the birds, and her bower, a cozy retreat in the woods!

The boys had not as yet been able to add very much to the family fortunes. Frances and her sisters did not mind worn-out frocks and scanty meals, but they were troubled to see their dear little mother so worried. The girls decided that something had to be done immediately.

"How wonderful it would be," thought Frances, "if an editor would buy one of my stories!"

She was only fifteen years old, and she did not know how to send a story to an editor. She had read in a magazine that contributors must write very clearly on foolscap paper, and enclose stamps.

Not having sufficient money with which to buy stamps and paper, Frances and her sisters earned the money by selling wild grapes.

At last the story was sent, but it was done secretly, for Frances was afraid that her brothers would tease her. What a happy day it was when, on its second trip, the story, together with another, brought a check for thirty-five dollars! She had found a way to help.

Frances Hodgson went on writing and selling her stories. Soon her books became famous. When she married Dr. S. M. Burnett, she was able to help him complete his education by her writing. Their son, Vivian, is also a writer. He has been a journalist and is the author of several books.

Mrs. Burnett has written many novels for grown people as well as stories that children love. *Little Lord Fauntleroy*, the tale of a lovable little American boy who won the heart of his crusty old English grandfather, is the best known of her books for children. Among her other well-known books are *Editha's Burglar*, *Sara Crewe*, *The Cozy Lion*, *The Secret Garden*, and *Land of the Blue Flower*.

Mrs. Burnett does not preach in her delightful stories for children. One can, however, easily see in her stories the lessons in thoughtfulness and courtesy she had learned from her mother. Frances Hodgson Burnett's great gift of imagination, together with her desire to write, enabled her to give us stories that have brought pleasure to many people.

KATHARINE BEMENT DAVIS—
THE GIRL WHO HAS HELPED
TO STRAIGHTEN TWISTED LIVES

THE villain had received his just deserts, but he, or rather she, was smiling with satisfaction. Her play, for Katharine was the author as well as a principal actor, had been a great success. Nobody had forgotten a line, and, in addition, the scenery had added a realistic setting. Who would ever have dreamed that the deep forest and bold cliffs were only boughs cut from the shrubbery, and boxes covered with mother's old gray shawl?

The back parlor of the Davis home was crowded with a friendly audience of girls and boys and a few mothers and fathers. This attendance was very gratifying to Katharine, for it assured her that the receipts would be large. With them she intended to provide a bountiful Thanksgiving dinner for a good woman who was having difficulty in supporting her crippled grandson.

Little did this merry eleven-year-old girl think that the work of helping others, begun in such a small way that night, was the work that she was to choose for her own later on. When she grew up she became a sociologist. This is simply a long word for a person who thinks, studies, plans, and works to help people lead happier, healthier, and better lives.

Katharine Bement Davis was born in Buffalo, New York, January 15, 1860. Within a short time the family moved to Dunkirk, New York. In the happy childhood days spent in this town on Lake Erie, there was

no hint of the sorrow of life which Katharine was to cheer in later years.

Besides four younger sisters and brothers
for playmates, Kitty, as she was called, had
no end of school chums. They were always
welcome at her home, for the Davis house
was a sort of center of good times for the
neighborhood. In the winter the children
acted plays in the house; in the summer time
they played Indian in the backyard, or built
houses of kindling wood.

Kitty was usually chief builder, because
she loved to watch something grow under
her hands. Making things was always such
a joy to her that years later, when she had
charge of the Bedford Reformatory, she
taught her girls how to do all sorts of useful
tasks. They even laid the concrete walks between the buildings.

This little Lake Erie girl had as great an
appetite for finding out how other people
did things as for doing them herself. Once
when a friend of the family took her for a
drive, she inquired the name and use of

every part of the carriage. By the time they reached home, her companion felt as if he had been put through a severe examination; but Katharine knew all about the carriage. This habit of going to the very bottom of things was to be of great use to a woman who was to have hard problems to settle in her public life.

Kitty Davis was very fond of reading. Her sisters and brothers often found her deeply absorbed in a book. Some of Scott's and Dickens' novels were among the book friends that she made at eleven and twelve years of age.

Little Katharine Davis liked to create with her mind as well as with her hands. When she was eleven years old, she had thought out tunes for a number of hymns. She enjoyed her music lessons, especially the part which showed her how music is made. The grown-up Katharine Davis realized that music helps people to forget their troubles and to think better thoughts. For this reason, she made sure that her girls at the reformatory should not only hear good music but should sing it themselves in their own glee club.

In the Davis family lived Grandmother Bement, a woman who had always had a hand in any new movement to make the world better. Katharine and the other children loved to hear her tell about the escape of slaves by means of the underground railroad, the fight against drink, and the struggle for rights for women. It was not strange that the granddaughter of such a woman should have a desire to be of service to the world.

The years flew on until Katharine Davis was ready for college. Business reverses had come to Mr. Davis, and he told his daughter that he could not pay her expenses.

"Never mind," answered Katharine, "I will earn them myself."

She kept her word. Studying by herself while she was teaching science in the Dunkirk High School, Katharine Davis completed two years of college work. She then entered Vassar College as a junior. She successfully passed the many special examinations that it was necessary for her to take. Upon the completion of two years' work at college Katharine Davis was graduated with honors.

For a number of years, Miss Davis spent her time, first, in teaching; then, in settlement work; and later, in further study. After three years of graduate work, the degree of Doctor of Philosophy, with honors, was conferred upon her by the University of Chicago. Thus she was ably prepared to enter the field of social service.

When it was announced that a new reformatory for women was to be opened at Bedford, New York, Dr. Davis was immediately interested. She thought that there she might be able to carry out her ideas for helping girls who had not had a pleasant home and wise parents like her own.

Dr. Davis received the appointment as superintendent of this reformatory, and set about getting acquainted with her girls. She believed that many of these lives that had been started in the wrong way might turn out happily, if some one took the trouble to study them.

Dr. Davis endeavored really to know the girls at Bedford. She was vitally interested in their welfare and did everything that she could to help them. She spent many successful years as superintendent of this reformatory.

Dr. Davis' ability to grasp a situation and meet it was clearly demonstrated at the time of the Messina earthquake. She was in Sicily when the disaster occurred, and immediately set about to aid the sufferers. Her work of rehabilitating the earthquake victims was so important that it won for her a Red Cross Medal, presented by President Taft.

When Dr. Davis took charge of all the prisons in the city of New York, as Commissioner of Correction, she had another opportunity for continuing her wonderful work. Katharine Bement Davis has served on a

number of commissions formed for the purpose of social betterment. Many persons
who desire to learn the best ways of working
for humanity go to her for advice. Because
of the little girl who carried into later life
her joy of working and her habit of investi-
gating things, many twisted lives have been
straightened.

GRACE HOADLEY DODGE —
THE GIRL WHO WORKED
FOR WORKING GIRLS

A GROUP of prominent men and women were sitting in the drawing room of a beautiful home in New York City, talking earnestly. Close by them sat a young girl, the eldest daughter of the house. She shyly added only an occasional word to the conversation, but she gave very careful attention to everything that her elders said.

One member of this group was Dwight L. Moody, the famous preacher. The girl listened to him with particular interest, and was deeply impressed by all he had to say.

There were often such gatherings in this home. No matter with what subject the conversation started, sooner or later came the question of how to help men and women lead the best kind of lives. It was not strange, then, that one day this young girl went to her mother and said, "I have found out what there is for me to do. I am going to help people."

That is exactly what Grace Dodge did. She helped people. Perhaps you will be surprised to learn that she helped each one of you girls and boys.

Every girl who has learned in a cooking class how to bake a wholesome loaf of bread; every boy who brings home from school a well-finished footstool for his mother, has Grace Dodge to thank. Every one of your older sisters who enjoys a swim or a game of basketball at the Y. W. C. A. has her to thank too. Of course, there are others to thank as well, for every good work needs many helpers.

When Grace Dodge was young, girls and boys in the public schools were not taught how to work with their hands; and girls who were earning their own living had no pleasant clubs. Grace Dodge believed strongly in these things, and worked so earnestly all her life for them that other people became interested too, and gladly cooperated with her in her beloved work.

Grace Hoadley Dodge was born in New York City, May 21, 1855. The Dodge family divided their time between their city home and their beautiful country house at Riverdale on the banks of the Hudson. Here Grace had many a fine gallop through the country with her brothers. Aside from these lively rides, which she greatly enjoyed, she lived quietly.

Even as a child, Grace thought very little about her own pleasure or herself. She liked to talk with the workmen who kept the beautiful lawns and gardens in order, and to make friends with their children. Although there were nurses and governesses in the family, the younger sisters and brothers always preferred to go to sister Grace when they wanted to be comforted; and they did not go in vain.

When Grace went shopping in the city with her mother, she used to think that it was very hard for girls to have to stand behind the counter all day. "I am ashamed to have so much while these girls have so little," she would many times say to herself, wondering what she could do about it.

Grace Dodge attended a private school at Farmington, Connecticut. After her school days were over, she began to do the work that had always interested her. One of the reasons that she accomplished so much was that, whenever she saw a need for anything, she set about to fill it. Furthermore, she kept persistently at the work until it was done.

Miss Dodge soon discovered that many of the girls in whom she was interested had to work long hours in factories. She began to find that they did not know much about

cooking, or sewing, or taking proper care of
their health. It was a great pity, she
thought, that these girls, many of whom
would soon be having homes of their own,
should know so little about the important
work of home-making.

Miss Dodge began to gather a group of
these girls about her every week, and talked
to them. She told them in a friendly, simple
way how to choose their clothes, how to keep
well and strong, and how to use their money
wisely. She told them, too, how to live the
right kind of lives and of the help that God
would give them. Often she talked to them
about the homes that they might make some
day.

The girls were eager to tell her about
themselves. Each one felt that she could
consider Miss Dodge as her personal friend.
"The Irene Club," as this group was named
after a beloved member, grew until it had
to be divided. Still the girls continued to
come. In this way clubs for working girls
were started. These clubs have proved to be

so successful that they have never stopped growing.

At that time, there were no places where girls who were busy all day could learn home-making. Miss Dodge, therefore, together with several other young women, organized classes for these girls in various household subjects. Miss Dodge and her associates soon discovered that there were very few teachers who had been trained to teach in this particular field. They later found that there was a lack of highly trained teachers in practically all of the departments of teaching.

Miss Dodge began to think that there should be a school to train teachers in the various branches of learning. It was not Grace Dodge's way to stop merely with thinking. She began to work for this school, and, largely because of her efforts, Teachers College of Columbia University rose on Morningside Heights in New York City.

Every year this college sends out thousands of men and women prepared to teach all the school subjects. The wonderful work that Teachers College is accomplishing is due, in a large measure, to the inspiration and guidance that Grace Dodge gave to the college throughout her life.

In many other ways Grace Dodge carried on her work of helpfulness. She was the first woman to serve on the Board of Education of New York City. Because of her pity for women and children who were unprotected and bewildered in travel, she organized the Travelers' Aid Society. So firm was her belief in what the Young Women's Christian Association does for girls that she worked to make it a strong organization. She was the president of its national board for eight years.

Miss Dodge often called herself "a working girl whose wages were paid in advance." Her money meant to her merely a means for doing good.

Grace Hoadley Dodge was unselfish and determined to fill the need that she saw. Through her efforts, school girls and boys now have many opportunities to use hand and brain together. It was because of her great interest in others that she brought joy into the life of many a wage-earning girl and helped to fit her for her work of home-making.

ALICE CUNNINGHAM FLETCHER —
THE GIRL WHO BEFRIENDED
THE RED MAN

ONCE upon a time there lived a little girl named Alice, who loved to sit upon the shore and listen to the song of the waves. She also liked to climb a high hill and look far off at the blue sky and the green slopes.

At home she had plenty of good books to read, and she loved them too. They told her delightful stories about things that had happened long ago. Sometimes she did not quite understand all that they said, as she read them curled up by the fire, but later, when she wandered in the woods, their meaning became clearer.

It was the same way when she played on the piano at home. The music set her to dreaming, and called forth puzzling thoughts. Outdoors she seemed to understand better what the music had to tell her.

This little girl was Alice Cunningham Fletcher. She was born in Boston, Massachusetts, in 1845. As she grew older, the thought came to her that if she felt so happy out in the open, how must the Indians feel who had lived a free out-of-door life for generations.

Gradually she began to think that these people, whom the world called savages, must have learned something about how to live happily. Alice Fletcher resolved that, if ever there came a time when it was possible, she would go to the home of the Indians and try to discover their secrets.

Meanwhile she studied all that books and museums could teach her of the story of the

Red Men. At last, there did come a day when she decided to go and live among them. It meant leaving behind her, beloved libraries, fine concerts, beautiful pictures, and even a comfortable bed and easy chair. Miss Fletcher felt, however, that there was something that meant more than comfort to her. It was the doing of a definite piece of work that she believed would be useful to the world.

Therefore, she left the friends with whom she could talk of books, pictures, and music, and went to live among the Dakota and Omaha Indians. From the door of her rude wigwam of buffalo skins, she could watch the little Indian children at play and see the everyday life of the older members of the tribe.

Most people think of the American Indian as a reserved, stern sort of person who never laughs or jokes. What Miss Fletcher saw from her wigwam gave her an entirely different opinion. She saw the Indians enjoy fun, and take a wide-awake interest in everything that went on around them. She decided that the sternness of the Indian was only a kind of mask that he wore before strangers.

Soon the New England woman ceased to be a stranger to her Indian neighbors. The love that they both had for the sky, the wind, the streams, and the forest helped to make them understand one another. It was not long before these children of Nature realized that Miss Fletcher had come to them as a friend; and that she was really interested in them. So they dropped their mask of reserve and let her know them as they really were.

Miss Fletcher, always a lover of music, became greatly interested in the music of the Indians. She found, however, that it was very difficult to study. An Indian does not sing just to be heard, but to express some feeling. His singing is a kind of prayer. It was only stray bits of such music that she was able to overhear and write down.

Then Miss Fletcher had a severe illness

which turned out to be a blessing, in one respect. When her Indian friends discovered
that she really wanted to hear their music,
they gathered about her bed and sang for
her. To please her, they even were willing
to sing into a phonograph, which was to
them a strange machine. Thus their songs
were preserved for all time. Miss Fletcher
has written a book entitled *Indian Story and
Song from North America*. This book has
already suggested themes for a number of
American musical compositions.

Presently a chance to prove that she was
really a friend of the Indians came to Alice
Fletcher. Some greedy white men were trying to get the good land away from the Red
Men, giving them poorer land in return.
Sometimes the Indians were so enraged with
their treatment that they would rise in re-
volt. The situation kept growing worse and
worse. Miss Fletcher realized that it would
be no better unless each Indian secured from
the government the right to hold a portion
of the tribal land for himself.

She set out for Washington to try to persuade Congress that the Indians must hold
their land just as the white man holds his. A
book which had just appeared, written by
Helen Hunt Jackson, called *A Century of
Dishonor*, helped a little to make people realize the wrongs done to the Indians. However, the congressmen were much more interested in the affairs of their own people
than in the Indians. Miss Fletcher, therefore, had to plead their cause continually until the Indian Land Act was finally passed.

The President asked Miss Fletcher to undertake the difficult task of allotting the
tracts of land to the Omaha Indians. He
knew that they trusted her and would be
content with her judgment. Later she did
the same work for other tribes of Indians,
to the satisfaction of everybody.

The Girl and Boy Scouts and the Campfire
Girls have interested Miss Fletcher very
much, because she believes that the outdoors
can bring health and happiness to girls and
boys. She has made a collection of Indian

games for these organizations. Also, Miss Fletcher has written books and articles about the Indians. Her writings are a great help to those who are making a special study of the different people of the world.

Alice Cunningham Fletcher gave up luxury and even comfort to learn about the Indians. The work of her mind has been of great value to learned people in their study of races; and the work of her heart will never be forgotten by the simple folk whose wrongs she helped to right.

LOUISE HOMER —
WHO BELIEVES THAT HARD WORK IS
THE SECRET OF HER SUCCESS AS A SINGER

LOUISE paid no attention to the calls of the children. What were a few hours' lost play compared with the treat in store for her! To-night after the regular prayer meeting, a song service was to be held to study hymns. Louise had begged so hard to be allowed to attend that her father had consented, provided that her lessons were thoroughly prepared in the afternoon.

These midweek song services were held at the Minneapolis church of which her fath-

er was pastor. There, Louise Beatty sang
for the first time outside her own home.
Little did this girl realize that her rich, deep
voice would later make her famous throughout the world.

Louise Dilworth Beatty was born in Pitts-
burgh, Pennsylvania, in 1872, into a family
where playing and singing were as much a
part of the daily program as eating or sleeping. Every one of the eight Beatty children
loved music. They were always singing in
duets, trios, quartets, or choruses.

Gathered around the fire on winter evenings, the family formed an impromptu orchestra. One sister played the piano; a
brother, the bones; Mr. Beatty, the flute;
and Louise, the future great opera singer,
the triangle.

Music had always delighted Louise, in
particular. At school, the seven-year-old
girl was stirred day after day by the thrilling notes of the music which the teacher
played as the pupils marched out for recess.

When Louise was fourteen years old, she

made her first appearance in public as a soloist. The church in the little Pennsylvania town where the family was then living was to give the cantata, *Ruth and Naomi*. Mrs. Beatty was rather amused when Louise was asked to take the part of Ruth, for she had never sung alone; but Louise herself was delighted. The rehearsals were a joy.

On the night set for the cantata, just as the singers were assembling, the disturbing news came that the man who was to sing the part of Boaz had missed his train. What was to be done! "I will sing his part too," offered Louise. She carried the basso-profundo part, in addition to her own, with such success that everyone told her mother that Louise's voice was wonderful, and that it should be cultivated.

Soon after this Louise began to take singing lessons, but the thought of becoming an opera singer did not occur to her. She kept busy with her high-school work, and later on studied music in Philadelphia. She also sang in a church there.

Then one day Louise Beatty took the most important step in her life. She decided to go to Boston to study music seriously. She felt that she must know more about music itself, if she were to become a real singer. She was advised to study harmony and composition with Sidney Homer, well known as a writer of music. She began her lessons with Mr. Homer, and, in addition, studied singing with William L. Whitney.

In 1895 Louise Beatty and Sidney Homer were married. Mr. Homer believed that his wife's voice was unusual, and that it was especially suited for opera. He wanted her to go abroad to train herself to be an opera singer. Accordingly, they went to Paris, where Madame Homer studied very hard for two years. She was able to do a tremendous amount of work without injuring her health, because she lived quietly and ate good home food at regular hours.

Then came the reward of the long hours spent in singing with her teachers, in practicing, and in studying languages and dramatics. Madame Homer was ready to sing in opera. In America, she appeared for the first time in San Francisco in the opera *Aida*, and a few weeks later in New York in the same part. She was a success at once.

For many years Louise Homer has delighted American audiences with her beautiful contralto voice. To keep her voice in good condition, and to learn the many parts that she has sung has not been an easy task. Every day during the season she practices and studies. Madame Homer believes that a great name, once made, can only be kept by thorough work.

While Madame Homer has never slighted any part of the work of her profession, neither has she neglected the work of home-making. She has always found time to be an intelligent and affectionate mother to her children and to preside over a real home. Remembering her own happy childhood, she has been determined that her children should have as much love and care and good training as her own mother gave her.

Louise, the eldest daughter, has a good mezzo voice and has sung in recitals, sometimes with her mother. Sidney, the second child, has also inherited musical ability.

Madame Homer and her husband have always been intensely interested in each other's work. The wife loves to sing the songs her husband composes, and he in turn takes delight in dedicating them to her. Louise Homer possessed a remarkable voice, but her own painstaking and constant work has brought it to perfection.

HARRIET GOODHUE HOSMER—
THE GIRL WHO LOVED ART
MORE THAN EASE

BATS, birds, toads, snakes, and beetles filled the room. Some were stuffed and mounted, and the others were either dissected or preserved in alcohol. This room was neither a museum nor a boy's den. It was owned by a little girl known as "Happy Hatty," and she, herself, had collected and prepared every one of its strange ornaments.

At the time that Harriet Hosmer was young, dissecting animals was not consid-

ered a proper amusement for a girl. The
neighbors thought that Harriet would have
been much better employed in sewing a fine
seam.

Harriet's father, an eminent physician,
had his own ideas about bringing up his little girl. Dr. Hosmer wanted her to live in
the fresh air and sunshine so that she would
be strong and healthy. The more Harriet
ranged the woods in search of specimens, the
better her father was pleased.

Dr. Hosmer gave his little girl a boat, so
that she could row on the Charles River,
which flowed past her home. He had a Vene-
tian gondola made for her, too, with velvet
cushions and a silver prow. In fact, he
thought that no gift was too rich for his
little girl, so long as it would keep her in the
open air.

Harriet enjoyed out-of-door life. She
grew tall and strong. Her muscles became
firm from much rowing. She could walk
miles without being tired, and was a fearless
rider. Thus, unknowingly, did this little

girl, who later became a distinguished sculptor, lay a strong foundation for her life work.

Harriet Goodhue Hosmer was born in Watertown, Massachusetts, on October 9, 1830. Even as a child she liked to play with clay and mold it into shapes. In one corner of the garden there was a clay-pit. Here the little girl used to go, when she grew tired of books, to fashion dogs and horses from the wet clay.

Harriet went to school in Watertown, and later attended a private school at Lenox, Massachusetts. After three years at Lenox, Harriet returned home. She then began to study drawing and modeling in Boston. Often she walked both to and from her lessons, a distance of fourteen miles. By this time, Harriet Hosmer realized that nothing made her happier than to turn formless bits of clay into beautiful objects. She felt that she would like to go still further in her work; she wanted to see some of her ideas take shape in marble.

Harriet knew that a sculptor cannot fashion life-like figures of people or animals without understanding the position and shape of the bony frame under the flesh. The decorations of her museum-like room, all those specimens that she had dissected or mounted as a child, had given her a fair start in the study of anatomy. She also studied this subject with her father. However, she realized that, if she were to be a real sculptor, she must know more about anatomy. She consequently looked about for a school where she might study.

The Boston Medical School would not accept this eager young student because she was a girl, but Harriet Hosmer was not a person to be daunted by one refusal. She was finally admitted to the St. Louis Medical College where she had a very thorough course in anatomy. After she had completed this course, she returned home and began to work seriously in a studio which her father had fitted up for her in his garden.

A beautiful girl representing Hesper, the

evening star, was the subject that Harriet
Hosmer chose for her first original statue.
From a solid block of marble she had a work-
man knock off the corners. As he was not
accustomed to working for sculptors she did
not allow him to go within several inches of
the part that she was to cut. All the rest of
this difficult work she did with her own small
hands.

For eight or ten hours a day she chipped
away at the block with chisel and a lead-
en mallet weighing four pounds and a half.
Muscles made strong and flexible by much
rowing and other exercises enabled her to
keep up this hard work day after day. The
block of marble was finally turned into the
head of a lovely maiden, her hair entwined
with poppies and a star on her forehead.

Beautiful as was this head of Hesper,
Harriet Hosmer felt that she must study
more. She was very desirous of entering
the studio of John Gibson, a noted English
sculptor who was then residing in Rome.
Now Mr. Gibson, hearing that Miss Hosmer

was young and rich, feared that she might
be easily discouraged before real difficulties.
However, as soon as he saw the daguerreo-
types of her "Hesper," the great sculptor
said to her father, "Whatever I can teach
her, she shall learn."

At the very beginning of her work with
Mr. Gibson, Harriet Hosmer showed him
that she was not the sort of girl who gives
up easily. The iron rod in a clay copy of the
Venus de Milo which she had modeled in
order that her teacher might have an idea of
her work snapped, and the figure fell to
pieces. However, without stopping to com-
plain, she started at once to make another
model.

Harriet Hosmer continued to work steadily with John Gibson. Then one day a message came from her father stating that he
had lost his fortune and could no longer send
her money. Miss Hosmer sold her fine saddle horse, and took an inexpensive room for
herself. Now she was actually to work for
her living.

Miss Hosmer became an important figure in the art and literary circles in Rome. She numbered among her friends the Brownings, Hawthorne, the Thackerays, and many other interesting people.

In the years that followed, many a beautiful statue emerged from unshaped marble through the transforming touch of Harriet Hosmer's hands. Her statue "Puck" shows a merry little elf, sitting cross-legged on a toadstool, his left hand resting upon a lizard, his right, clasping a beetle. Some of her other important statues are "Œnone," "Beatrice Cenci," "Sleeping Faun," and a statue of Thomas H. Benton. "Zenobia in Chains," which is in the Metropolitan Museum of Art, is the most famous of all. This is a colossal statue, representing the beautiful Queen of Palmyra taken prisoner by the Roman Emperor Aurelian.

Harriet Goodhue Hosmer so loved to watch beauty grow under her fingers that she was willing to give up the care-free, easy life that she might have had as the child of a rich man. Because she developed her talent through hard, serious work, she won for herself a high place among the sculptors of America.

JULIA WARD HOWE—
WHOSE BATTLE HYMN SANG ITSELF
INTO THE HEARTS OF A NATION

IN the days when New York was not the
big city that it is now, there was a fash-
ionable section called the Bowling Green.
The people who lived there often used to see
a great yellow coach roll by. Within, three
little girls sat stiffly against the bright blue
cushions. These children were dressed in
blue coats and yellow satin bonnets to match
the chariot and its lining. They were the
three little Ward children, one of them, Julia,
to be known later throughout the land as

Julia Ward Howe. She is the author of the famous patriotic hymn which you sing so often at school, the "Battle Hymn of the Republic."

Julia Ward, the eldest of the three little girls, was born in New York City, May 27, 1819. Although her father was a rich man and loved his children very dearly, they did not have many of the pleasures which most children to-day enjoy as a matter of course.

The Ward girls had very little chance to romp and play outdoors and get acquainted with the birds and flowers. To be sure, they went to Newport, Rhode Island, in the summer, but poor little Julia had to wear a thick green worsted veil to protect her delicate skin. It was not until she had children of her own that she realized how much she had missed in her youth. She was glad that her children could live close to Nature.

Julia was, however, a happy child in spite of her rather sober life. She was alone much of the time, for her lively brothers were away at school and the two younger sisters played by themselves; but she was never lonely. She read a great deal: Shakespeare, Byron, and as much other poetry as she could find. She enjoyed her music and other lessons.

Julia was particularly fond of study. At first she had lessons at home, but at the age of nine she was sent to a private school nearby. Here this little girl studied a difficult book, Paley's *Moral Philosophy*, with girls of sixteen and eighteen years of age.

Once, at this time, she heard a class reciting an Italian lesson. The musical sound of the language delighted her, and she listened whenever she had the chance. She secured a grammar, and studied it by herself. Then, one day, she handed the surprised teacher a letter, written correctly in Italian, asking permission to join the class.

Julia loved to make up poetry, and when she was in her thirteenth year, she copied a number of her poems into a brown blank book as a present for her father. One of them was a poem written about her mother,

whom she had lost when she was only six
years old. Still another was in French; and
in the four stanzas there was only one mis-
take.

The study of languages was always a delight to her. She spoke and wrote French
and German very well. Later in life she
studied Spanish, and at the age of fifty she
did not feel that she was too old to begin the
study of Greek.

At twenty-four years of age Julia Ward
married Dr. Samuel Gridley Howe. He was
a noble-hearted man whom everyone knew
as the first person to teach language to a
blind deaf mute, namely, Laura Bridgman.

A happy, busy time began for these two
people, who believed that life should be lived
for others. Dr. Howe was engaged with his
work for the blind and for the freeing of the
slaves. Mrs. Howe went on with her studies,
and wrote poems, plays, and essays. She
helped her husband with his antislavery
work, and together they edited a newspaper
called the *Commonwealth*.

Yet no matter how crowded these days were, there was always a time in the afternoon that was set aside for the children. The mother played and sang to the little folks, and there were merry romps, as the father, wrapped in a big fur coat, played bear and growled fiercely. Both mother and father often read aloud to their children.

When the Civil War broke out, Julia Ward Howe longed to help her country and soon a special way came. One day, she was driving back into Washington with friends, after having witnessed a review of some troops. Their carriage was delayed by the returning soldiers. To pass away the time, Mrs. Howe and her companions began to sing war songs. Among them, they sang,

"John Brown's body lies a-mouldering in the grave."

"Why do you not write some good words for that stirring tune?" someone asked Mrs. Howe.

"I have often wished to do so!" she answered.

The next morning Mrs. Howe awoke before dawn, and found the words of a song shaping themselves in her mind. As soon as the poem was complete, she rose and, in the early morning light, wrote it down on a sheet of paper. This poem was the famous "Battle Hymn of the Republic," which soon sang itself into the hearts of the nation.

Mrs. Howe's writings have been numerous. In addition to her books of poetry she also wrote much in behalf of social reforms. She lectured far and wide, and loved to talk to school children. Because she wanted women to learn how to help themselves, she founded, or helped to found, many clubs and organizations for them. She wanted them to have the vote too.

Mrs. Howe's children have followed in their mother's footsteps and written books themselves. One of her daughters, Laura E. Richards, has written delightful stories for children. Her book, *Two Noble Lives*, tells very beautifully the life stories of her remarkable mother and father. Maud Howe

Elliott and Florence Howe Hall are also the authors of many books. The son, Henry Marion Howe, has written books on scientific subjects.

Our country honors Julia Ward Howe as the author of one of its greatest songs, which will ever continue to stir our patriotism. Because as a girl she made the best use of her talents, she was enabled to fill a long life with great service.

HELEN KELLER—
THE DEAF AND BLIND GIRL WHO FOUND
LIGHT AND HAPPINESS THROUGH KNOWLEDGE

IN a beautiful southern garden where
birds sang gaily and roses, honeysuckle,
and jessamine shed their fragrance, little Helen lay face downward on the ground.
She hid her hot cheeks in the cool leaves and
grass. The tears flowed fast. Why, why
would no one understand what she wanted?
Sometimes it seemed as if she could not bear
the world of darkness and silence in which
she lived. This little girl could not talk like
other children. Neither could she see the

yellow rose petals, nor hear the songs of the birds.

On June 27, 1880, Helen Keller was born in the little Alabama town of Tuscumbia. For nineteen months she was just like any other happy, healthy baby girl. Then a severe illness took away her sight and hearing, and, because she was unable to hear her baby words, she soon forgot how to talk.

One day when Helen was nearly seven years old, a new doll was put into her arms. Then, in her hand a lady made the letters *d-o-l-l* in the deaf alphabet. Helen did not know that things had names, but she was amused with this new game and imitated the letters for her mother. Helen's new friend and teacher was Miss Anne Sullivan. She had come from the Perkins Institution for the Blind, in Boston, to teach this little girl.

When the finger game had been going on for a month, Miss Sullivan spelled the word, *w-a-t-e-r*, into Helen's hand, letting her feel the water from the pump. A light broke over Helen's face. For the first time she understood that everything had a name. She touched the pump and the trellis, and asked for their names. In a few hours she had learned thirty new words. That night Helen went to bed very happy, looking forward, for the first time in her life, to another day.

A new, joyous life now began for this little girl whose mind had been in the dark. She soon realized that every word that she would learn would provide her with a new and pleasant thought. Miss Sullivan gave Helen slips of cardboard on which words were printed in raised letters. She never tired of playing the game of arranging these words in sentences.

Down by the river Helen built dams of pebbles and dug lakes and bays and was taught how the world is made. In the woods her teacher put a violet or dogwood blossom in her hand and explained about growing things. She learned to know the crickets and katydids by holding them in her hand. Helen played all these games, not realizing that she was learning lessons.

When Helen was eight years old, Miss Sullivan took her to Boston to the Perkins Institution for the Blind. The child was delighted to find there little girls and boys who could talk to her in the language of the hand. She enjoyed, too, the books in the library printed in raised type, and began to read in earnest. It was at this time that she climbed Bunker Hill Monument, counting every step. She had another lesson in history at Plymouth Rock.

It was difficult, of course, for Helen to talk with people who did not know the deaf alphabet. Miss Sullivan had to spell out the conversation into her hand. When Helen heard of a deaf girl who had been taught to speak, she was determined to learn too.

It was the hardest task that she had undertaken, for she could not hear the sound of her own voice nor see the lips of others. She would feel the position of her teacher's tongue and lips when making a sound, and then imitate the motions. Constant practice and the great desire to achieve always spurred her efforts. It was slow, tedious work, but Helen persevered.

She *did* succeed in learning to speak. It was a very happy day when Helen actually spoke to her parents and to her little sister Mildred.

At ten years of age Helen had put her whole heart and will into learning to speak. Six years later, after having studied lip-reading, French and German, and other difficult subjects, she determined to undertake what seemed like another impossibility. She made up her mind to go to college!

Many of the books that she needed were not printed in raised type. She could not hear lectures nor take notes. Such were a few of the difficulties that this young girl had to face. Nevertheless, Helen was not to be discouraged. She entered the Cambridge School for Young Ladies and bravely began her preparation for Radcliffe College.

Miss Sullivan went to Helen's classes with her and spelled into her hand all that the teachers said. Helen wrote her compositions on the typewriter. She used it, too, in answering successfully the examination questions.

Helen was urged to take special work at college, but she preferred to follow the regular course. Once more this blind and deaf girl conquered all the difficulties, and in 1904 was graduated from Radcliffe College. She had completed the same course as had the young women at Radcliffe College and the young men at Harvard University who could see and hear.

As Helen Keller grew older, she realized that knowledge, besides giving pleasure, enables one to be of more help in the world. After her graduation she was eager to be of service. Naturally, she thought of the blind first. Miss Keller was made a member of the Massachusetts Commission for the Blind and served on several boards for the blind and deaf. She has always urged that the blind be given the kind of education that will fit them to support themselves.

Miss Keller has written many magazine

articles and several books. When she was only twelve years old she wrote a short account of her life for the *Youth's Companion*. Her *The Story of My Life* was published before her graduation from college.

Instead of being a burden, this blind and deaf girl early became a happy, useful citizen. She has succeeded because she was determined to know more, no matter how much hard work it cost her. Helen Keller says that the worst darkness is ignorance. Her life motto has been: "Knowledge is love and light and vision."

MARIA MITCHELL—
THE GIRL WHO STUDIED THE STARS

IT was an eventful day in the Mitchell home. The parlor window had been taken out and the telescope mounted in front of it. Twelve-year-old Maria, at her father's side, counted the seconds while he observed a total eclipse of the sun.

Not every twelve-year-old girl could be trusted to use the chronometer, an instrument which measures the time even more accurately than a watch. Maria, however, had been helping her father in his study of the stars ever since she could count. Before many years this little girl beside the telescope became America's best-known woman astronomer.

On the little three-cornered island of Nantucket, off the coast of Massachusetts, Maria Mitchell was born, August 1, 1818. With its broad sandy beaches, its wide moors, and ocean breezes, the island was a delightful spot in which to grow up.

The Mitchell home was a pleasant place, filled with the laughter and fun of a large family of children. Due to the mother's careful planning, the wheels of the household machinery ran very smoothly. No one would have guessed, by seeing the cheerful, comfortable home, how far Mrs. Mitchell had to stretch a tiny income.

Work and play were happily mingled. Little Maria, with her sisters, learned to cook and sew. Maria was always ready to do her share of the household work. If she swept a room, she did it thoroughly. When she arranged the furniture it might not be done artistically, but every piece was straight.

She could not bear to have things crooked. This exactness about little things was one of the qualities that made it possible for this girl to become a great astronomer.

There were always good books in the Mitchell home. They were read over and over, and were very carefully handled. One textbook, an algebra, was used by eight children in succession, each child adding his name inside the cover.

Mr. Mitchell, who was a Quaker, enjoyed quoting to his children from the Bible and from the poets. He was particularly fond of references to his beloved stars. He often said that an astronomer could not fail to believe in God. One of the earliest poems that Maria learned was about the heavens, beginning, "The spacious firmament on high." She used to like to say it over to herself when in later years she was frightened or troubled.

The most unusual object in Maria's home was her father's telescope. On pleasant evenings it was set up in the back yard. Ever since boyhood Mr. Mitchell had been in-

terested in the stars and had made astronomy his special study. Every clear evening
he observed the heavens. Maria was always
glad to help him. Soon she took as keen a
delight in watching the sky as he.

The chronometers of all the whale ships
which sailed into Nantucket were brought
to Mr. Mitchell to be "rated," as it was called.
Maria used to help her father with this; and
at a very early age learned how to use a
measuring instrument called the sextant.

There was no school at this time where
Maria Mitchell could be taught astronomy.
Even Harvard University had no better telescope than her father's. Maria, however,
had an excellent teacher in him. Many scientists sought out Mr. Mitchell in remote Nantucket, and Maria had the benefit of their
conversation.

The years of Maria Mitchell's girlhood
passed quietly but happily. She went to two
schools that her father taught, and then to a
private school where she did very good work
in mathematics. At sixteen years of age she

began to teach. She gave up teaching, however, to become librarian of the Nantucket Athenæum, a position that she held for nearly twenty years.

The library was open only afternoons and Saturday evenings. In the afternoons there were few visitors, so Miss Mitchell had plenty of time for reading and study. She went on with her studies in higher mathematics and worked out difficult astronomical problems. Whenever visitors came in and chatted, as they liked to do with this bright, interesting young woman, her book was dropped for knitting. Maria Mitchell never wasted a moment.

Every clear evening was spent on the housetop observing the heavens. No matter how many guests there were in the parlor, Miss Mitchell would slip out and, lantern in hand, mount to the roof where the telescope was now kept.

On October 1, 1847, there was a party at the Mitchell home. Maria, as usual, ran up to the telescope. Presently she hurried back and told her father that she had seen a new comet. Mr. Mitchell was convinced that she was right and he wrote to Harvard University, announcing the discovery. Maria Mitchell received for this discovery a gold medal offered sixteen years before, by the King of Denmark, to the first discoverer of a telescopic comet. This won world-wide distinction for Miss Mitchell.

The next year another great honor came to the Nantucket girl. She was elected to the American Academy of Arts and Sciences. She was the first woman to be admitted to this important scientific society.

Soon after this Miss Mitchell was asked to put her knowledge of astronomy to use on a work for navigators called the *American Nautical Almanac*. She was to watch the course of the planet Venus, and to make the tables which mariners need to guide them. For nineteen years she kept up this important work.

It was quite natural that a woman who had watched ships pass her island home ever

since childhood should long to travel. Miss
Mitchell was especially eager to meet the
great scientists of Europe. At last the
happy time came for a European trip.
Everywhere she was cordially received, and
astronomers not only opened their observa-
tories to her, but welcomed her in their
homes.

Shortly after Vassar College was opened,
Maria Mitchell was asked to become its professor of astronomy and director of the ob-
servatory. Accepting this position meant
giving up to a great extent her own studies
and the hopes of making more discoveries
in the heavens. However, Miss Mitchell was
very anxious that women should have a
chance for higher education. Therefore, she
put her own ambitions aside and threw herself into the work of teaching.

Hundreds who knew her at Vassar will
say that she chose wisely. She was honored
as a remarkable teacher and loved as a friend
and adviser.

Miss Mitchell was a prominent member of

many important organizations. Several colleges conferred degrees upon her.

In 1905 Maria Mitchell was elected to the Hall of Fame. This hall, which is situated on the grounds of New York University, was built to commemorate the achievements of distinguished citizens of the United States.

Maria Mitchell lives in the memory of scientists as a great astronomer. She lives in the hearts of her students as one who taught the beauty of thorough and accurate work, and of lives free from pretense and sham.

ALICE FREEMAN PALMER —
THE GIRL WHO GUIDED COLLEGE GIRLS

MR. Freeman lifted his five-year-old daughter to the platform to speak her piece. Little Alice had been allowed to go comfortably to sleep during the earlier part of the village entertainment. However, as soon as she was on her feet, all traces of drowsiness disappeared. She loved the bit of poetry that she had taught herself. With rosy cheeks and sparkling eyes, she declaimed it so enthusiastically that the whole roomful of people burst into delighted clapping.

Seeing smiling faces all about her, Alice smiled, too, and put her little hands together and clapped as vigorously as anyone. She did not realize that it was she herself who had given the audience pleasure. Because these friends and neighbors were happy, she was happy with them.

When she grew up, Alice Freeman could still forget herself and enter into the moods of others. She seemed to know exactly how the other person felt. That was one of the reasons why, when she became the president of Wellesley College, she was able to help the students make the very best of their lives.

This first public appearance of Alice Elvira Freeman was in the country village of Colesville, New York, where she was born, February 21, 1855. Her father was a young farmer, high-minded and hard working. Her mother was a farmer's daughter and had been a school teacher. Both parents were very deeply religious.

Mrs. Freeman was so busy cooking and churning and washing that five-year-old

Alice helped her all that she could. She washed dishes, gathered eggs from the barn, and looked after the three younger children.

Two years later there was even more need of Alice's help. Mr. Freeman had decided to become a doctor, and his young wife had bravely undertaken to carry on the farm alone while he was studying. The two little sisters and the brother depended on Alice to fasten their buttons and to amuse them. Thus from a very early age Alice Freeman had to think for others as well as for herself. Such training was of great value to her when she had to care for a large family of Wellesley College girls.

When Alice's father began to practice medicine in the village of Windsor, New York, Alice loved to drive with him and hold the horse during his visits to patients. She was interested in hearing about his cases and she enjoyed the shady roads and wayside flowers. Throughout her whole life, she rejoiced that she had been a country child.

At ten years of age Alice Freeman became
an eager pupil at the Windsor Academy.
One of her teachers, who had taken a great
interest in her throughout her course, in-
spired Alice to go to college.

When Alice talked the matter over with
her father, he said that he could not afford
to send her to college. He felt that, as there
was only money enough for one college education in the family, the boy must have it.
Alice begged very hard to go. She promised
to send her brother through college, and to
give to her sisters whatever education they
desired. Dr. Freeman at length consented
to her entering the University of Michigan.
As for her promise, she kept it to the letter.

At the University Alice was confronted
with her next big problem. She failed to
pass her entrance examinations! The President had already talked with the earnest,
intelligent seventeen-year-old girl. He realized that her school, though a good one, had
not prepared her for college. Therefore he
asked the examiners to allow her to enter on

a six weeks' trial. At the end of that time, there was no doubt of Alice Freeman's ability to lead her classmates.

This frail girl made up all the studies required for entrance, did excellent work in her classes, and took an active part in the college clubs. She went to church twice on Sunday and attended a midweek service. She taught a Sunday-school class and put new life into the Christian Association. She was never too busy to be friendly, cheerful, and joyous.

Alice Freeman received her Bachelor's degree after four years of college work. Three years later, after having taught successfully in the middle west, she was asked to become the head of the history department at Wellesley College. In 1881, when she was only twenty-six years old, Miss Freeman was made its president.

As college president Miss Freeman led a very busy life. The college was young and needed to be guided carefully. She worked so lovingly and enthusiastically for it that more students applied than could be admitted. Wealthy people gave money for scholarships, and many new schools were started to prepare students for college.

Miss Freeman was a real mother to the large family of Wellesley College girls. They were free to go to her with all their problems, and they never went in vain. She had a way of seeing the best thing in a girl and of making her feel that she must bring the whole up to this level.

After six years of this devoted service to Wellesley College, Alice Freeman was married to George Herbert Palmer, then Professor of Philosophy at Harvard University. Happy years followed for them. Mrs. Palmer was as successful a home-maker as she had been a college president. She was a delightful hostess to the many interesting guests that were welcomed at their home.

Mrs. Palmer still found plenty of work to do for others. She was a trustee of Wellesley College, a member of the Massachusetts State Board of Education, and the president of the International Institute for Girls in Spain. She always could find time for any cause which was to make the world wiser and better.

From all over the country Mrs. Palmer's advice was sought on whatever had to do with education. Many colleges and universities conferred degrees upon her. In 1920 her name was greatly honored by being selected for the Hall of Fame.

Alice Freeman Palmer, college president and great educator, never lost the child Alice's gift of sympathy. She cared very deeply what people did with their lives. That was why she could inspire them to be of real service.

MAUD POWELL —
THE GIRL WHOSE VIOLIN SPREAD AFAR
THE MESSAGE OF MUSIC

THE sweet strains of one of Mozart's violin sonatas filled the room. One of the players was a bright-eyed little girl. The other, it was easy to guess from the proud and tender look that she gave her little companion, was the child's mother. Both mother and daughter loved these hours together with their violins.

Music meant much to this mother. She enjoyed composing as well as playing. She was very happy to know that music gave pleasure to her little daughter also. The hope was in this mother's heart that some day little Maud would be a great musician. It was a hope that was realized, for, in later years, Maud Powell became known as the foremost American violinist.

Maud Powell was born in Peru, Illinois, August 22, 1868. When she was two years old, the family moved to Aurora, Illinois, where, for several years, her father was head of the public schools. From the time that little Maud was a baby she loved music. When she was only four years old, she was taught to play simple pieces on the piano.

At an early age she showed such fondness for the violin that Mr. and Mrs. Powell decided to have her study in Chicago with Mr. William Lewis. Twice every week little Maud had to travel on the train, forty miles each way, to take her lessons. She had to go alone, too, because money could not be spared to pay the fare of a companion. The little musician enjoyed these lessons very much. After she grew up she did not forget this teacher, and often said that he had given her a splendid foundation for her work.

Before she was ten years old, the little violinist played in public as a soloist with the Chicago Ladies Vocal Quartet. By the time that she was twelve years old, it was quite evident that Maud Powell had real talent for the violin. Then, her parents decided that their little girl must be given the best possible musical education. They fully realized that this would be very expensive, and would necessitate a long absence from home.

One day Maud said good-by to her dear father and all her young friends, and sailed away to Germany with her mother to study music. Mr. Powell missed his little girl and her mother very much, but he was proud when he received letters telling of his daughter's success. The good news helped him to work harder so as to be able to send them the necessary money.

After studying at Leipzig, the little American girl passed a brilliant examination, and was chosen to play at a public concert.

Later, Mrs. Powell was anxious to have her daughter study with a distinguished French teacher, Charles Dancla, at the Paris Conservatory. Maud learned that there were only a few new pupils to be admitted and that she would be one of eighty applicants. The examinations were made especially severe for foreigners, but Maud Powell was the first to be admitted.

This Frenchman delighted in teaching the eager young American girl. He took great pains with her, and was always just and fair. After having had but three lessons on a selection on which a class of eighty-four was to be examined, Maud Powell passed above everyone else. One of the pupils had been studying this selection for six months. It was not only Maud Powell's greater talent but also her general knowledge of music that made it possible for her to grasp new work readily.

The lonely father at home was cheered by messages of his young daughter's success and popularity in London, where she was playing in drawing-rooms and at concerts. Joachim, a distinguished German violinist, was so impressed by Maud Powell's playing that he wanted her to join his class in Berlin. He said that she was more than a mere talented child; that she would, with training, make a great artist. She passed the examinations for his class, without the usual six months' preparation, and worked hard with him for a year.

Then came the longed-for return to America and the reuniting of the family. Maud Powell was eager to show her father that his sacrifices had not been in vain. Many people thought that the violin was an instrument for a man only. Nevertheless, at the age of seventeen, this young girl made her debut as a violin soloist at a concert of the New York Philharmonic Society, conducted by Theodore Thomas. From that time on the fame of Maud Powell's violin grew. It was heard throughout the United States and in many foreign lands.

Miss Powell did not play merely for a livelihood or for fame. Music had meant so much to her that she felt that she must bring it into the lives of others. She was especially eager to give the inspiration of her music to people who had few opportunities of hearing great artists. That was why she gave recitals in hundreds of small towns, and was always glad to play for schools and colleges.

Miss Powell never slighted her programs even though she was playing in the smallest place. She gave her best, thinking that some one in her audience might not have another opportunity to hear good music.

In fact, Miss Powell never gave anything but her best at any concert. She would memorize a long selection perfectly even if she knew it were to be played only once. She took great pains to have her programs varied, and delighted in introducing American compositions to her audiences.

In 1904 Miss Powell married H. Godfrey Turner. He assisted her greatly by attending to the business arrangements for her concerts.

Great praise and appreciation came to Maud Powell for the marvelous music that she brought forth from her violin. However, the road from gifted childhood to finished artist was a long, hard one. She pushed aside every obstacle by her tireless work. The long hours of practicing and the years of homelessness and loneliness were endured for the sake of her beloved music. Maud Powell will always be remembered, not only because she played the violin remarkably, but because she carried the message of music to out-of-the-way parts of the world.

ELLEN H. RICHARDS —
A SCIENTIST
WHO HELPED HOME-MAKERS

"A HALF pound of saleratus, please," demanded a customer. "I never can cook with soda." "Give me baking soda," another woman insisted. "I cannot use saleratus."

The bright-eyed young girl behind the counter of the country store supplied them both from the same package, rather amused that they should not know that baking soda and saleratus are as alike as two peas in a pod.

"I should like to know more about the nature of the things that I am selling," thought Ellen Swallow. Little did she dream that her future years were to be spent in making life easier and happier for women by enabling them to learn about these very things.

On December 3, 1842, Ellen Henrietta Swallow was born near the village of Dunstable, Massachusetts. She was an out-of-door girl and loved to follow her father and uncles about the farm. She drove the cows to pasture, rode horseback, and often pitched hay. She made a little flower garden too, and tended it carefully.

Little Ellen was also quick and skillful at indoor tasks. Her mother, who had a deft hand at any kind of housework, taught her to sew and cook. Ellen's doll's bed had sheets and pillowcases daintily hemstitched by her own hand. At the country fair, one year, two prizes fell to thirteen-year-old Ellen Swallow, one for a beautifully embroidered handkerchief and another for the best loaf of bread.

Ellen's mother and father were well educated, and had been teachers. They taught Ellen at home until she was ready for the academy.

Mr. Swallow gave up farming and opened a country store in the village of Westford, Massachusetts, so that Ellen could attend the academy there. Ellen enjoyed her studies and mastered them thoroughly. She was such a fine Latin student that later she was able to earn money for her college expenses by teaching that subject.

Ellen Swallow was as active and energetic out of school as in school. She was a capable little business woman. She waited on customers in her father's store and kept his accounts. She even made trips to Boston to buy goods for the store. This early training was very helpful when in later years she had to handle large sums of money for many philanthropic and educational purposes.

At home Ellen was often the housekeeper for weeks at a time, during her frail mother's illnesses. She not only cooked and washed, but she cleaned house, papered rooms, and laid carpets, as well. What she learned of managing a house in her school-girl days was a very valuable addition to what science taught her later about good home-making. Ellen Swallow was very quick and capable. In addition to her school, home, and store duties, she had time for reading and for working in her precious flower garden.

After her academy days Ellen Swallow's hours were filled by teaching a country school, helping in the store and at home, and caring for sick friends and neighbors; but she was not satisfied. She felt a great longing to learn and to do more.

There was no college in New England at that time which admitted women. Ellen Swallow therefore decided to enter Vassar College, at Poughkeepsie, New York, which had only recently been founded.

College days were very happy ones for this active-minded young woman. She wrote home to her mother glowing accounts of her new life and told her all about her school work and the books that she was reading. Science was her favorite study. One of her teachers was Maria Mitchell, who took a great interest in the young girl.

After graduating from Vassar College, Ellen Swallow was eager to go on with the study of chemistry that she had begun there. After some difficulty she gained admittance to the Massachusetts Institute of Technology, as its first woman student. In fact, she was the first woman to enter any strictly scientific school in the United States. One of the teachers thought that this young woman looked rather frail to be taking such difficult work. The President answered, "Did you notice her eyes? They are steadfast and they are courageous. She will not fail."

Not only did she *not* fail in her studies, but she also supported herself. She did tutoring, took charge of an office for a friend, and temporarily ran the boarding house where she lived.

It was feared about this time that the

water near many towns and cities in Massachusetts was becoming unfit for drinking.
The newly organized State Board of Health
decided to have samples of the water examined to see whether it contained impurities.

Miss Swallow had proved herself to be so
accurate and dependable that the chemist
chosen to analyze the water handed over
most of the work to her. Often she had to
work far into the night when many samples
came in at a time. She analyzed forty thousand samples of water. This careful work
meant the prevention of much disease. For
ten years she was assistant chemist for the
State Board of Health, and then chemist for
ten years.

When Ellen Swallow was married to Professor Robert Hallowell Richards, head of
the department of mining engineering in
the Massachusetts Institute of Technology,
she did not give up her public work. Yet she
maintained a real home in which she carried
out her ideas about building and furnishing,

cleanliness and fresh air, and labor-saving devices. Many guests were welcomed to this busy woman's home and all found it a place of restfulness and peace.

Mrs. Richards' great desire was that girls should have the same opportunity to receive a scientific training as had boys. Largely through her efforts a Woman's Laboratory was opened in connection with the Massachusetts Institute of Technology. This Laboratory was established for the purpose of giving scientific training to women.

Mrs. Richards gave generously to the Laboratory, teaching without salary, and contributing to its support as well. Soon after women were admitted to the Institute on the same footing as men, Mrs. Richards was made Instructor in Sanitary Chemistry in the Institute, a position which she held for the rest of her life.

Mrs. Richards might have spent her time in scientific research. However, she preferred instead to put her knowledge of science to practical use. She tested wall papers and fabrics to see if they contained arsenic, and staple groceries to detect impurities. She studied oils to discover how the danger from explosives could be lessened.

Mrs. Richards wrote many helpful books about home-making. She organized a society of people interested in promoting right living in the home, the school, and the community. The name of this organization is American Home Economics Association. Because of her influence home economics is now taught in schools throughout the land.

To Ellen H. Richards, sanitary chemist, the facts of science were never just facts, but the means of making people healthier and happier.

ELIZABETH CADY STANTON —
THE GIRL WHO HELPED TO DRAFT
WOMAN'S DECLARATION OF INDEPENDENCE

"WHAT a pity it is she's a girl!"
Four-year-old Elizabeth heard
this remark over and over again
from the visitors who had come to see her
baby sister. She thought that she ought to
feel sorry for the baby, too. When she was
a little older, Elizabeth Cady realized what a
pity it was that girls and women could not
have the same privileges and advantages as
had boys and men.

Elizabeth Cady was born at Johnstown,

New York, November 12, 1815. When this
little girl grew up, she called the first Woman's Rights Convention and worked all her
life to gain more privileges for women. As
a child she felt the disadvantages of being a
girl in the early days of the 1800's.

When her only brother, a fine promising
college graduate, died, eleven-year-old Elizabeth realized that her father loved his son
far more than all of his five daughters.
Longing to comfort him Elizabeth climbed
on his knee.

"Oh, my daughter, would that you were a
boy!" was all that he could say.

From that moment Elizabeth resolved
to equal boys. To be learned and courageous she decided was the way to accomplish
her purpose. Before breakfast the next
morning she went to her dear friend and pastor and asked him to teach her Greek. She
insisted on beginning that very minute. To
prove herself courageous she learned to
drive a horse, and to leap a fence and ditch
on horseback.

Within a short time she began to study
Greek, Latin, and mathematics with a class
of boys at the village academy. She did so
well that she won the second prize, a Greek
testament. Joyfully Elizabeth rushed home
expecting to hear her father say, "Now, you
are equal to a boy." However, his kisses and
praise failed to take away the sting of his
remark, "Ah, you should have been a boy!"

Elizabeth's father was a distinguished
lawyer and judge. His office adjoined the
house, and there his little daughter spent
much of her time talking with his students
and listening to his clients.

Often his clients were widows who wept
and complained that the property which they
had brought into the family had been willed
to their sons. Elizabeth could not understand why her father, who was wise and
kind, could not help these poor women. Then
Judge Cady would take down from the
shelves a big volume and show her the law.

The students, seeing how interested she
was in the laws about women, amused them-

selves by reading to her the most unfair laws that they could find. They often teased her, too, in order to hear her bright remarks.

Little Elizabeth was so distressed by the unfairness of the law in regard to women that she made up her mind to cut them all out of her father's law books. She refrained from doing this upon learning that it would not help the situation.

Much to her disgust Elizabeth Cady could not go to college, as did her boy classmates, for at that time girls were not admitted. However, she entered the Willard Seminary for girls in Troy, New York, where she studied for some time. Later she went on with her studies at home, never losing her interest in laws for women.

In her twenty-fifth year Elizabeth Cady married Henry B. Stanton, a lecturer on antislavery, who later became a lawyer. After several happy years in Johnstown and Boston, the young couple settled in Seneca Falls, New York. By this time the champion of woman's rights began to know by experience something of a woman's home problems. She had a big house to manage with very little help, and her lively girls and boys needed constant care.

In her round of everyday duties, however, Mrs. Stanton did not forget the wrongs to women. She, together with Lucretia Mott and some others, called a big meeting, the first Woman's Rights Convention, at Seneca Falls in 1848, to talk over this question.

At this meeting Mrs. Stanton and her coworkers presented a Declaration of Sentiments based upon the Declaration of Independence. They also presented eleven resolutions, one of which demanded the vote for women. Mrs. Stanton was entirely responsible for this resolution and placed great emphasis upon it. She believed that through the ballot for women all other rights for women could be secured.

The newspapers made a great deal of fun of all the reforms discussed at the convention, particularly the proposal that women should vote. In those days most people were quite ready to admit that a woman could manage her home capably and be bright and entertaining in company. However, they thought it very unwomanly that she should dream of helping to make laws to secure better schools or cleaner streets.

Mrs. Stanton was surprised and distressed to have her very serious purpose treated so lightly, but ridicule did not prevent her from upholding woman's rights whenever she had an opportunity.

Three years after this she met Susan B. Anthony, the woman who was to be her lifelong friend and fellow-worker. Except for their lectures in the cause of temperance and antislavery, Mrs. Stanton and Miss Anthony gave their whole lives to gaining more freedom for their fellow-women.

The two friends were very different in characteristics, but they were of one mind on the question of woman's rights. Miss Anthony had not at first thought it necessary for women to have the vote, but she was soon won over to her friend's opinion. Year after year these two earnest workers endeavored to arouse the country to do something for women. Never a jealous thought as to which one should have the glory for anything accomplished marred this fifty years of friendship.

Mrs. Stanton and Miss Anthony lectured in big cities and all sorts of little out-of-the way places. Together with their friend Mrs. Gage, they wrote a very complete history of what had been done to gain the vote for women.

Of Mrs. Stanton's children, a daughter, Mrs. Harriot Stanton Blatch, has followed directly in her mother's footsteps as a public speaker for the cause of women. She has also written several books about woman's place in the work of the world. Theodore Stanton, one of the sons, also writes in behalf of women.

Throughout a long lifetime Elizabeth Cady Stanton courageously and steadfastly pleaded the cause of women. She lived to see them enjoying better property rights and educational privileges, and in four states helping to make the laws. Eighteen years after her death the Nineteenth Amendment gave the vote to women throughout the United States.

HARRIET BEECHER STOWE —
THE GIRL WHOSE STORY OF SLAVERY
AROUSED THE WHOLE WORLD

IT was the night of the annual exhibition
of the Litchfield Academy. Twelve-year-
old Harriet Beecher waited eagerly for a
certain part of the program. Presently she
heard read before all the learned people as-
sembled the familiar words of her own composition, one of the three chosen for this
great occasion.

As Harriet listened to the sentences that
she had composed with so much care, she
watched the face of her father who sat on

the platform. It brightened. She knew that he was interested.

At the close of the entertainment she heard him ask, "Who wrote that composition?"

Her teacher replied, "Your daughter, sir."

It was the proudest moment of Harriet's life. When this little academy student became a woman she wrote a book which set the whole world to thinking of the evil of slavery. It was *Uncle Tom's Cabin*.

Harriet Beecher was born at Litchfield, Connecticut, June 14, 1811. Her father had only a country parson's meagre salary to provide for the wants of eleven children. What a father he was—grave and serious enough in the pulpit, but full of fun and enthusiasm at home. It was mere play for Harriet and the boys to pile wood, when their father superintended.

Harriet was very rich in sisters and brothers. She loved them all dearly, especially the merry, energetic big sister, Catherine, and the chubby little boy two years younger than

she, Henry Ward Beecher, who grew up to
be a famous minister.

Little Harriet had only a sweet memory
of her mother who had died when she was a
small child. Wherever she went, she was
told of her mother's beautiful life. It made
her very happy to know that she had a mother whom everyone loved.

There were no expensive toys in the Beecher family, but Harriet was well content without them. She played with her glass-eyed
wooden doll and a set of cups and saucers
made by her own hands out of codfish bones.
In the woodpile she found treasures in the
moss and lichens on the logs. From them she
fashioned little pictures using the moss for
green fields, sprigs of spruce for the trees,
and bits of glass for lakes and rivers.

Some of Harriet's happiest hours were
spent curled up in a corner of her father's
study, surrounded by her favorite books.
It was a peaceful, restful place, she thought.
She liked to glance up at her dear father as
he was writing or thinking over his sermons.

She enjoyed looking at the friendly faces of
the books on the shelves. Very few of them,
however, were books that she could understand.

One day while rummaging in a barrel of
old sermons in the attic, Harriet came upon
a copy of the *Arabian Nights*. How she and
her brothers pored over its pages! Another
precious treasure discovered in a barrel was
Shakespeare's play, *The Tempest*.

Harriet's delight in stories was satisfied
in another way. Every fall it was the cus-
tom to make enough apple sauce to last for
the winter. It took a whole barrelful for the
big Beecher family. All the little fingers
were pressed into service to peel or quarter
apples. Mr. Beecher would then ask who
could tell the best story. As the apples bub-
bled and hissed in the big brass kettle, story
after story went around. Mr. Beecher, himself, recited scenes from Sir Walter Scott's
novels, which were then new.

In the unheated, barnlike meetinghouse
where Mr. Beecher preached, Harriet also

spent many happy hours, although she was cold and cramped from sitting through the long sermons. Usually she did not understand her father's big words, but one day he spoke so earnestly and simply about God's love that Harriet never forgot it.

When Harriet grew up, she married Calvin Ellis Stowe. He was a professor in the Lane Theological Seminary, in Cincinnati, Ohio, of which her father had become the president.

In Ohio, adjacent to the slave state of Kentucky, everybody was thinking and talking about slavery. The Fugitive Slave Law, whereby runaway slaves must be returned to their masters, was causing heated discussions. Mrs. Stowe and her husband believed this to be a very unjust law and they helped a colored girl, the "Eliza" of *Uncle Tom's Cabin*, to escape from her pursuers. Mrs. Stowe opened a school for colored children in her house, and raised money to buy the freedom of a slave boy.

Ever since the days of her school compositions Mrs. Stowe had enjoyed writing, and some of her stories had found their way into the papers. When Professor Stowe went to Bowdoin College, in Brunswick, Maine, to teach, his wife tried to do a little writing to add to his small salary. However, the work of looking after a large house and her family of small children left her little time for writing stories. Sometimes with her paper on the corner of the kitchen table and her ink on the teakettle, she managed to write a story, superintend the making of pastry, and watch the baby at the same time.

One day Mrs. Stowe received a letter from a relative urging her to write something that would stir the country against the evil of slavery. She earnestly declared that she would.

Soon thereafter the plot for her story, *Uncle Tom's Cabin*, flashed across her mind. She wrote a chapter as quickly as possible and sent it to the *National Era*, an antislavery paper. Chapter after chapter followed, written rapidly as the scenes of the story presented themselves to her. When it was completed it was published as a book. In a few days ten thousand copies were sold; in a year, three hundred thousand copies.

Mrs. Stowe wrote many other books, though none of them attained the prominence of *Uncle Tom's Cabin*. This book is considered to have been one of the most influential and widely read novels in literature.

From distinguished people all over the world came letters of congratulation to Mrs. Stowe. What she had written just because she felt that she must, with no thought of money or fame, brought her both. Harriet Beecher Stowe was further honored by being elected to the Hall of Fame in 1910.

Harriet Beecher Stowe's gift of expression, which she had been cultivating for many years under all sorts of difficulties, made it possible for her to draw a picture of slavery that aroused the whole world.

KATE DOUGLAS WIGGIN—
WHO PUT THE JOY OF LIVING
INTO HER BOOKS

ALTHOUGH Katie Smith loved all the books on the black walnut bookshelves, the ones that she took down most often were some fat volumes by Charles Dickens. So much did she enjoy these stories that she named her yellow dog "Pip" after a character in one of them; and across her sled in big scarlet letters were painted the words "The Artful Dodger."

One day Katie's mother read in the paper that Mr. Charles Dickens had come to America. When Katie heard that he was going to give a reading from his books in Portland, Maine, only sixteen miles away, she was very much excited. How she longed to see and hear the wonderful man who had created so many delightful characters!

Katie and her mother had planned to go to Charlestown, Massachusetts, for a visit, stopping overnight in Portland. Now Katie's mother decided that they would leave home so as to be in Portland on the night of the reading. But alas! a grown-up cousin, instead of little Katie, was taken to hear Mr. Dickens.

Katie bore her disappointment as best she could, and the next day after the reading she received her reward. Who should be riding on the very same train with Katie and her mother, but the great Charles Dickens himself! While Katie's mother was talking with an acquaintance, the little girl slipped into the empty seat beside her favorite author.

"Where did you come from?" inquired Mr. Dickens in a surprised tone of voice.

"I came from Hollis, Maine," stammered Katie Smith.

Presently the little girl and the famous author were chatting away like old friends. Mr. Dickens chuckled when he heard about the naming of Katie's dog and her sled, and his eyes grew moist when she spoke of the characters that made her cry.

This nine-year-old admirer of Dickens had not the slightest idea that one day she would be an author herself. Years later, however, when she was known as Kate Douglas Wiggin, she wrote a delightful story about another little State-of-Maine girl, entitled *Rebecca of Sunnybrook Farm*. She also wrote many other enjoyable books.

Kate Douglas Smith was not a State-of-Maine girl by birth. She was born in Philadelphia, September 28, 1859. When she was six years old her family moved to the village of Hollis, Maine.

Little Katie Smith loved the world in which she lived and especially her own little corner of it on the banks of the Saco River.

What fun she had with her little sister Nora and her playmate Annie. Nora is better known to us as Nora Archibald Smith, the author of many charming stories for children. These little girls gathered velvety pussy willows, hunted for arbutus in the early spring, and picked wild strawberries and raspberries in the summer.

How amusing Katie found the froggery, a nice quiet pool where lived her favorite frogs! She knew them all by name and twice a week she arranged them very gently in a row on a strip of board for a singing lesson. In the winter she enjoyed coasting and snowballing. She also liked to be in the house where she could play with her orphanage of paper dolls and read her beloved books.

To little Katie Smith, work was almost as amusing as play. It was fun, she thought, to cut up rhubarb for sauce, to make milk toast for supper, to water the plants, to iron the handkerchiefs, and to go for the milk. Just to be alive, to run along the river bank, to help about the house, was enough for this joyous child. No dreams of authorship had come to her, though she was filling her mind with the pictures which she was later to give to the world in her books.

Katie Smith was taught at home and also attended a district school. Later she went to a boarding school in Maine, after which she attended Abbot Academy in Andover, Massachusetts, from which she was graduated.

When Kate Smith was seventeen years old she followed her family to Santa Barbara, California, where they had gone several years before. As there was very little money in the family treasury, the elder daughter of the house felt that she must begin to help at once. A girl's story which she had written merely to amuse herself she decided to send to a magazine editor. What was Kate's delight to receive in payment for the story a check for one hundred and fifty dollars, which came just in time to pay some taxes!

The proud young author, however, did not think of writing for a living. She decided that she did not yet know enough to write. She realized that she must live a little longer and learn more. In the meantime she decided to find some useful work to do. Years later, after she had become a successful author, she said that this decision was the most sensible act of her life.

Kate Smith soon found the work that she sought. Kindergartens were still very new in America. Miss Smith studied the system and organized a free kindergarten in San Francisco, the first one to be established west of the Rockies. This young woman was very successful in bringing happiness into the lives of the little children who flocked to her kindergarten.

It was for the purpose of raising money for kindergartens that the young teacher wrote two stories, *The Story of Patsy*, and *The Birds' Christmas Carol*. She had them printed and sold at twenty-five cents a copy. Miss Smith thought that the only reason they sold well was because so many friends were anxious to help the good cause of free kindergartens. Little did she realize that these books would later bring her fame.

In 1880 Kate Douglas Smith married Samuel Bradley Wiggin, who was a California lawyer. It was not until several years later that Mrs. Wiggin thought of sending a paper-covered copy of *The Birds' Christmas Carol* to a publisher. This charming story of the Ruggles family was accepted at once and more stories requested. From that time on Mrs. Wiggin devoted herself to writing.

Girls and boys of to-day all over the world love her Rebecca, Carol, Patsy, and Timothy just as the little girl of Hollis, Maine, loved the children in Dickens' stories. Kate Douglas Wiggin wrote often for children because she loved them and never forgot what it is like to be a child. She has also written many very entertaining books for older people.

"Rebecca" is not, as some people have thought, small Katie Smith herself. However, the district school where Rebecca wrote her famous composition was the one that the author attended.

In Kate Douglas Wiggin's books are many pictures of the life that she lived as a child. She put herself into her books, but not as a character. In her stories you will find something of her own quick wit, her cheerfulness, her satisfaction in doing and helping, and her joy of living.

THE EAGLE'S NEST
BEWARE!

FRANCES E. WILLARD —
THE GIRL WHO FOUGHT
THE DRAGON, DRINK

FRANCES called her brother Oliver's attention to the new law that she had written the previous night for "Fort City." It read: "We will have no saloons or billiard halls, and then we will not need any jails."

This little girl's favorite game was to plan a play city, a place where everyone could live happily. She took a special delight in making laws for the health and pleasure of the citizens of her city.

Planning the city was only play, but in this game as well as in all others Frances Willard showed her remarkable ability as an organizer. Little did she realize that years later this ability would make her a valuable leader of the Temperance Cause.

Frances Elizabeth Willard was born at Churchville, New York, September 28, 1839. When she was but a tiny child, her parents moved to Oberlin, Ohio, in order that they might study at the university. After a few years of happy student life, Mr. Willard was obliged to give up his books and his dream of becoming a minister for a life outdoors in the West.

What an adventure the journey was for the three little Willards! There were no fine Pullman trains in which they could travel, for there were no railroads in that section of the country in those days. Three clumsy prairie schooners carried them to their new home. Frances and her little sister Mary rode in the third, perched comfortably enough among the cushions on the top of their father's old-fashioned desk. For three weeks they traveled over the prairies, stopping only to cook their meals, gypsy-fashion, and to rest on Sundays.

"Forest Home" was the name given to the pretty rustic cottage that Mr. Willard built among the oaks and hickory groves, by the banks of the Rock River, near Janesville, Wisconsin. It was a delightful place in which to spend a happy childhood. To be sure, the Willards' only callers at first were the chipmunks and birds, but there were no dull days. Every minute was filled. Frances did her share of the household tasks and far more than her share in planning the family games.

Although the lively Frances was the leader in all the fun, there was one sport in which she was not allowed to join. This was horseback riding. Confiding to her brother that she *must* ride something, she tried the cow. Her father laughed when he saw her on her clumsy steed, and allowed her to have a horse after that. This simple way of disposing of difficulties served her well all her life.

Active and full of fun as Frances Willard
was, she liked to be quiet and thoughtful too.
A black oak in the garden bore the sign:
THE EAGLE'S NEST — BEWARE!
High up in the leafy branches Frances would
sit for hours, making up bits of verse or edit-
ing the "Fort City" newspaper.

On Sunday afternoons the children would
wander with their mother in the orchard
while she talked to them about the beauty
that God had created. They realized that
God was very near.

Frances was quite young when she first
heard from her parents of the unhappiness
that drink brings. With the other children
she signed a pledge written in the big family
Bible, and ending:

"So here we pledge perpetual hate
To all that can intoxicate."

For some years Mrs. Willard took charge
of the children's lessons, but later a young
woman from the East came to teach them
and some of their little neighbors. No child
was ever more hungry for knowledge than

little Frances Willard. She often declared
that she wanted to learn everything.

There came a day when Frances was very
happy and excited. A little schoolhouse had
been built in the woods about a mile away.
It was so small and brown and plain that she
called it "a sort of big ground-nut," but it
was a real schoolhouse, with a Yale graduate
for a teacher.

Later on Frances and Mary went away to
college. They attended Milwaukee Female
College, and then Northwestern Female College at Evanston, Illinois, from which they
were graduated. At these two schools energetic, high-spirited Frances was a leader,
both in and out of the classroom.

Frances Willard was the same earnest,
hungry-minded, determined girl when she
became a teacher that she had been as a
student. She began to teach in her own
"brown-nut" schoolhouse during her first
college vacation. After her graduation
from college she spent a number of years
in the teaching profession. During this time

she was at the head of several important
schools. She concluded her teaching career
as Dean of the Woman's College in Northwestern University.

About this time many people were becoming alarmed at the amount of drunkenness
throughout the United States. They were
distressed by the misery caused by drink. In
the small towns in the Middle West, women
often marched through the streets singing,
praying, and begging saloon keepers to give
up their business.

In Chicago a band of women, marching to
the City Council to ask to have the Sunday
closing law enforced, were rudely treated by
the mob. Frances Willard had never forgotten the pledge that she had signed in the
family Bible. The insults to these women
aroused her fighting spirit. She felt that she
must help.

One day the mail brought her two letters.
One letter offered her the principalship of a
prominent school in New York City, which
would pay her a large salary. The other let-

ter asked her to become president of the Chicago branch of the Woman's Christian Temperance Union. Because of the meager funds of this organization no salary was offered her. Although she had no means besides her earnings, Miss Willard chose the latter position. Later, discovering that she had no private income, this organization provided a sufficient salary for her.

Frances Willard felt sure that she should devote her life to the cause of Temperance. The Woman's Christian Temperance Union needed a leader badly, so with all the energy with which she had planned her play city, Miss Willard developed this organization.

From that time on, Frances Willard gave her whole life to the Cause. She pleaded eloquently for Temperance in every large city in the United States and in many small ones. She became the president of the National Woman's Christian Temperance Union, and later of the World's Woman's Christian Temperance Union, which was organized through her efforts.

In the National Capitol there is a hall where each state may place the statue of two of its most beloved leaders. Illinois erected there the first statue to a woman—a marble figure of Frances E. Willard. In the year 1910 Frances E. Willard's name was selected for the Hall of Fame.

To-day, we have that for which Miss Willard dreamed and worked: a nation in which the sale of intoxicating drinks is prohibited by law. The passing of this milestone on the road to Temperance has greatly benefited the world. To Frances E. Willard, who contributed so much to the success of this movement, humanity is indebted.

Ella Flagg Young—
Whose Slogan Was
"Better Schools for Girls and Boys"

"WHAT does that mean, Ella?" The boy lifted his eyes from his weeding as he put the question to his sister. Ella, seated on a chair between the garden rows, rested her open book on her knees a moment and sat thinking. Then, choosing her words carefully, she explained what she had just read aloud.

"Oh, I see now," the boy exclaimed. "Go on."

Ella resumed the reading.

Ella Flagg was in poor health as a little girl, so her mother chose gardening as the best means of keeping her outdoors. Ella found that while her fingers were busy pulling weeds, down one long row and up another, her active little mind was eager to be busy too.

She and her brother decided to combine reading and gardening. The plan worked well for these two children, as it relieved the weeding hours of monotony. Ella then made the discovery that whatever she tried to explain she must first understand very clearly herself. It was in this way that Ella Flagg Young, who became a famous educator, did her first teaching.

For the first thirteen years of her life Ella Flagg lived in Buffalo, New York, where she was born January 15, 1845. On account of ill health she was not allowed to go to school with her sister and brother. Her mother and father believed that there would be plenty of time for regular lessons when her body had grown stronger.

She was eight or nine years of age before she learned to read and then she taught herself. One morning Ella's mother was reading in a newspaper an account of a fire. Ella was so much interested that she took the paper and tried to read the article. She remembered the exact beginning, but she did not know any of the other words. With some help, however, she was finally able to read the entire article.

Even though this little girl did not have regular lessons, there was much to be learned in a home such as hers. Mrs. Flagg was an energetic, capable woman. She was skillful in managing household affairs and much in demand among her friends and neighbors, when there was sickness or trouble in their homes.

From her mother, Ella learned how to settle household problems for herself. Because of this training she was able always to look squarely in the face the big problems that confronted her, when she was at the head of the Chicago school system.

Little Ella could learn a great deal, too, merely from hearing her mother and father talk, for they were thoughful, intelligent people. Mr. Flagg had had to leave school when he was only ten years old to be apprenticed to the sheet-metal trade. However, by reading and study he had educated himself.

Sometimes Ella used to go to her father's shop and sit for hours watching him at work at his forge. She asked questions about all the processes that he followed so that she really understood what he was doing. From these pleasant hours in the shop came her love of handwork and her interest in having it taught in the public schools.

When Ella began to go to school her father took a great interest in the way in which she studied. He had always done his own thinking and he did not want his daughter to depend on other people for hers.

Once Ella discussed with her father a drawing in her textbook of an hydraulic press that she was studying. She realized that he was displeased with what she said so she immediately decided to study the drawing more thoroughly. Soon she discovered that an important part had been left out. In the examination on the press the next day the papers of all the other students, who had blindly followed the book, were marked zero, while Ella's received a perfect mark.

Ella Flagg graduated from a Chicago high school and also from the Chicago Normal School. This ambitious girl began to teach when she was seventeen years of age. She first taught in a primary grade for six weeks and then in a higher grade where some of the pupils were larger and older than she. In a year she was made head assistant of the school and in two years principal of the practice school, where she helped to train the normal-school students.

Ella Flagg married William Young in 1868. However, she did not give up her work. She climbed steadily up the ladder of the teaching profession. Even though she had become very successful she felt that she needed more education. Consequently she studied at the University of Chicago from which she received the degree of Ph. D.

Mrs. Young became assistant superintendent of the Chicago schools, then professor of education in the University of Chicago. Later she was made principal of the Chicago Normal School, and finally superintendent of schools in Chicago.

As soon as Mrs. Young became superintendent of the Chicago schools she began to work for the children. She ordered the windows to be opened, top and bottom, in the schoolrooms to do away with the foul air produced by a poor system of ventilation. She organized fresh-air classes for pupils who needed an extra amount of oxygen.

She asked the teachers to help her improve the course of study. Handwork, in which the hours at her father's shop had given her an interest, she introduced into every grade. A new study, which she called "Chicago," brought the children into closer relation with their own city, teaching them its geography, history, and government.

The fame of Mrs. Young's work in education spread beyond her own city. The National Education Association, which had never had a woman in office, made her its president. Mrs. Young wrote many books about education.

When Mrs. Young was asked how she managed to accomplish so much, she always said that it was through systematic work. The first year that she began to teach, she planned to devote three evenings a week to study, three to seeing her friends, and Sunday evening to church.

For a long lifetime Ella Flagg Young worked to solve the problem of educating the girls and boys of Chicago and the nation. The clear and independent thinking that she had cultivated as a girl helped to give her a place as one of the great educators of our day.